LINGUISTICS|当代语言学研究文库|

魏耀章◎著

An Investigation into the Roles of Cognitive Ability and Language Proficiency in Chinese EFL Learners' Metaphor Comprehension and Production

认知能力和语言水平对中国英语学习者隐喻理解和生成的影响

上海交通大学出版社
SHANGHAI JIAO TONG UNIVERSITY PRESS

内 容 提 要

本书首先从隐喻研究以来最具影响的以 Aristotle 为代表的古典隐喻理论和以 Lakoff & Johnson 为代表的当代隐喻理论(Steen 2000: 261)入手,借助于其他相关研究成果,探究隐喻的本质属性。在此基础上,作者指出,两种理论的根本分歧不在于它们所讨论的隐喻本质有所不同,而是由于它们各自受当时所处的社会历史和学术环境的影响和制约,从不同的角度阐释了对隐喻的理解。

图书在版编目(CIP)数据

认知能力和语言水平对中国英语学习者隐喻理解和生成的影响 / 魏耀章著. —上海:上海交通大学出版社,2015

ISBN 978-7-313-13474-5

Ⅰ.①认… Ⅱ.①魏… Ⅲ.①英语-隐喻-研究 Ⅳ.①H315

中国版本图书馆 CIP 数据核字(2015)第 166925 号

认知能力和语言水平对中国英语学习者隐喻理解和生成的影响

著　　者: 魏耀章
出版发行: 上海交通大学出版社　　地　　址: 上海市番禺路 951 号
邮政编码: 200030　　电　　话: 021-64071208
出 版 人: 韩建民
印　　刷: 虎彩印艺股份有限公司　　经　　销: 全国新华书店
开　　本: 880mm×1230mm　1/32　　印　　张: 7.75
字　　数: 224 千字
版　　次: 2015 年 9 月第 1 版　　印　　次: 2015 年 9 月第 1 次印刷
书　　号: ISBN 978-7-313-13474-5/H
定　　价: 38.00 元

前　言

自 Aristotle 伊始，隐喻研究跨越了两千多年的历史长河，期间理论流派竞现，各有其说，仁智互见。由于外语教学研究界总是热衷于从理论语言学研究中获取养料（White 2003：147），因此这些隐喻理论无疑对外语教学研究的走向起着举足轻重的影响。有鉴于此，本书认为，当前对于外语教学研究和教学而言，要提高外语学习者的隐喻能力，首当其冲的问题是要对各种隐喻理论进行深入的分析，进而探究影响外语学习者隐喻能力发展的各种关键因素。

据此，本书首先从隐喻研究以来最具影响的以 Aristotle 为代表的古典隐喻理论和以 Lakoff & Johnson 为代表的当代隐喻理论（Steen 2000：261）入手，借助于其他相关研究成果，探究隐喻的本质属性。在此基础上，作者指出，两种理论的根本分歧不在于它们所讨论的隐喻本质有所不同，而是由于它们各自受当时所处的社会历史和学术环境的影响和制约，从不同的角度阐释了对隐喻的理解。换句话说，Aristotle 的隐喻理论正如 Kittay（1989）和 Mahon（2001）所说还是以认知为基础的，只是它更注重研究隐喻的修辞功能，而 Lakoff & Johnson 更关注隐喻作为人类认识世界之工具的认知功能。因此，隐喻能力从本质上来说是认知的问题。另外，依据 Richards（1965）的观点，隐喻能力并非像 Aristotle 所言是天才的标志；相反，人类普遍具有这种能力，所不同的只是“度”的问题，也就是说只是隐喻能力强与弱的问题。其次，本文认为，由于隐喻从本质上说具有认知的特点，一般来讲，由于本族语学习者的语言水平已经相对完善，因而对他们来说，语言交际过程中隐喻的理解和产出可能更多取决于认知水平。然而，对外语学习者而言，因其语言水平相对薄弱，其隐喻理解和生成能力除了受认知能力的影响外，语言水平也可能是一个不可忽略的制约因素。当然，本书也并不否认其他诸如学习风格、动机、文化背景等因素对隐喻理解和生成能力的影响。作者进而指出，由于外语学习者的认知能力和语言水平不同，其隐喻理解和生成能力也就不同。另外，一般而言，理解和生成是两个不同的认知过程，因此，认知能力和语言水平对二者的影响也可能呈现不同的情况。为了进一步探究以上问题，本研究从应用语言学的角度，以 82 名中国大学英语专业学生为被试对象进行了一项实证研究，得出以下主要结论。

1)中国英语学习者的隐喻理解能力既是一个认知能力的问题，又是一个语言水平的问题。研究发现，学习者的认知能力和语言水平与其隐喻理解能力高度相关；认知能力可以解释 43.6%隐喻理解能力的变异，语言水平可以预测 43.9%的相关变异。换句话说，认知能力和语言水平都是决定隐喻理解的显著变量。就隐喻生成而言，比较来看，认知能力对隐喻生成能力变异的解释力为 83.5%，而语言水平仅能解释其 10.8%的变异，但是却和其有非常明显正相关关系。可以看出，认知能力对隐喻生成能力的预测力明显强于语言水平。这一结果说明，隐喻理解和生成是两个不同的认知过程，因此，学习者的认知能力和语言水平在隐喻理解和生成过程中扮演着不同的角色。由此推理，对外语学习者来讲，隐喻理解既是一个认知能力的问题，也是一个语言水平的问题。而隐喻生成主要还是一个认知能力的问题，但是语言水平和其高度相关。

2)认知能力和语言水平在不同认知能力和语言水平的学习者隐喻理解过程中表现出不同的作用。具体而言，当学习者处于低水平认知阶段时，其认知能力对隐喻理解的解释力不明显，只达到 27.1%，而语言水平的解释力却非常明显，达到了 48.3%。当学习者处于高水平认知阶段时，认知能力和语言水平对隐喻理解的作用正好和其处于低水平阶段时相反。换言之，在学习者认知能力较高时，其认知能力对隐喻理解能力的预测力非常明显，达到了 44.4%，而这个时候语言水平的预测力并不明显，只有 6%。这说明，学习者的认知能力越强，其认知能力对隐喻理解的贡献越大，随之，其语言水平的贡献越小。但是实验发现，当学习者无论是处于哪个(高、低)认知水平时，其认知能力对隐喻生成的解释力都非常明显，而语言水平的解释力都不明显。这说明，隐喻生成主要还是一个认知能力的问题。

当学习者处于低水平语言阶段时，其认知能力和语言水平对隐喻理解的解释能力都非常明显。实验发现，在这一阶段，认知能力可以解释 54%隐喻理解能力的变异，语言水平能解释 34.4%的相关变异。当学习者处于高水平语言阶段时，认知能力对隐喻理解能力的解释力很明显，达到了 37.8%；而语言水平的解释力并不十分明显，只有 28.9%。这表明，语言水平越高的学习者更多的是借助他们的认知能力来理解隐喻，而语言水平低的学习者同时依靠其认知能力和语言水平来达到他们理解隐喻的目的。实验发现，对语言水平不同的学生来讲，其隐喻生成能力的高低主要还是取决于他们认知能力的高低，语言水平的作用不明显。这表明，隐喻生成不同于理解，主要是认知能力的问题。

3)实验发现，在理解四种不同的隐喻句子时，学习者的认知能力除了对第一种句子理解的预测力不明显外(20.7%)，对其他三种句子的预测力都比较或非常明显(分别为 22.9%，43%，42.3%)。而语言水平对所有类型的隐喻句子理解的预测力都非常明显(依次为 42.7%，41.2%，28.4%，29.4%)。具体来讲，当目的语和母语的概念和语词都对等时，认知能力对其隐喻理解能力的解释力不明显，而在其他三种情况下，即，当两种语言在概念和语词方面呈现出各种不同的差异时，认知能力能显著地解释学习者隐喻理解能力的变异。对于隐喻生成而言，学习者的认知能力对构成生成能力的三个变量：隐喻的数量、恰当性、新颖性的预测能力都极其明显，依次达到 75.5%，84.3%，76.8%，而语言水平的预测力都不明显。

本书最后讨论了本研究对于同类研究和外语教学和学习的启示意义，指出了其局限性以及今后同类研究的方向。

魏耀章
同济大学外国语学院
2015 年 3 月 10 日

List of Abbreviations

ARIT	Advanced raven intelligence test
APT	The degree of aptness of metaphors produced in the topic writing
CFTMS	Comprehension of the four different types of metaphorical sentences
CG	Cognition group
COG	Cognition
CTP	Creative thinking practice
EFL	English as a foreign language
ESP	English for specific purposes
FLTL	Foreign language teaching and learning
HCG	High cognition group
HPG	High proficiency group
HLG	High language proficiency group
ICG	Intermediate cognition group
ILG	Intermediate language proficiency group
LCG	Low cognition group
LG	Language proficiency group
LLG	Low language proficiency group
LP	Language proficiency
LPG	Low proficiency group
MAQ	Meta-cognitive ability
METACOG	Metacognition
MC	Metaphor comprehension
MN	The number of metaphors in the composition
MP	Metaphor production

NOV	The degree of novelty of metaphors produced in the topic writing
PDAN	Production of density，aptness and novelty
PER	Percentage
RLC	Recognition of linguistic cues
SRC	Sentence reading comprehension
SSF	Sentence stem filling
TEM 4	Test for English Majors Grade Four
TSA	The total score of aptness
TSV	Total score of vocabulary
TW	Topic writing
UDTM	Understanding of different types of metaphor

List of Tables

Contents

Chapter 1 General Introduction

1.1 Introduction

The study of metaphor has undergone quite a long history of over 2,400 years, during which a number of competing, if not all, conflicting theories about it have been advanced. The earliest research into metaphor can be traced back to about 300 B.C. Ever since then, we have witnessed a period when constant arguments about and unremitting efforts at metaphor have attracted the attention from a constellation of sciences, ranging from philosophy, anthropology, psychology, sociology, linguistics, neurology as well as pedagogy (Martinich 1990; Richards 1965; Searl 1978; Sperber & Wilson 2001; Gibbs & Steen 1997; Ortony 1998; Fitzgerald 1993; Hu 2002; Cameron & Low 2001; Low 1988; Goatly 2000; Lakoff & Johnson 1980; Littlemore 2001; Paul 1998; Boers 2000a, 2000b; Bailey 2003; Moser 2000; Guerrero & Villamil 2000; Rohrer 1995; Kimmel 2004). This boundless enthusiasm for metaphor reached its climax in 1970s, and thereby resulted in what Mark Johnson called a metaphormania in the academic circles (Yu 1998: 2; Chen 2003: 361) and became a topic of the utmost importance in cognitive science in 1990s. This was the situation in the western world. However, comparatively speaking, this phenomenon of the prosperity of and zeal for metaphor study in the outside world appeared to go, to some extent, if not at all, unnoticed in China (Shu 2003: 1) before 1990s. Thereafter, things seemed to turn out to be different. In the past fifteen years, papers on metaphor have been published in large volumes (Shu *et al* 2004). Nevertheless, a careful reading of these publications reveals that a big proportion of them is mostly focused on the ontological and psychological aspects of metaphor and a small, if not all, percentage are targeted on metaphor in language teaching and learning. This is especially true of the situation in foreign language teaching and learning (FLTL) not only in Chinese context, but also in the western world (Lindstomberg 1997; Low 1988; Bailey 2003: 5-6; Johnson 1999; Pang & Ding 2002: 9; Jiang & Zhang 2003; Cai 2005). Cameron & Low (1999: 77) makes it even clearer, "The study of metaphor has exploded in the last decades, but little of the impact of that explosion has so far reached applied linguistics." Although Cameron & Low are somewhat exaggerating, at least the problem has not received rapt attention of many of the FLTL researchers and practitioners.

And it is from these bare facts that the present research takes its initial inspiration.

1.2 Need for the study

As is stated in the above section, relatively little empirical research into metaphor has been conducted from the perspective of foreign language teaching and learning. However, with the rise and spread of cognitive linguistics, recently some researchers come to realize the importance of metaphor in language learning. In a sense, the realization of the importance mainly derives from some researchers' awareness of the pervasiveness of metaphor in everyday language. For example, it is found that about six metaphors turn up every minute in ordinary conversations (Kellerman 1998: 1) and most English speakers utter about 10 million novel metaphors per lifetime (Cooper 1999: 233).

Realization of this high frequency makes understanding and utilization of metaphor an essential part of language learning. Consequently, researchers, as Johnson (1994: 455) implies, very likely enlightened by Chomsky's linguistic competence (1965) and Hymes' communicative competence (1971), advanced another similar term, metaphorical competence (Danesi 1986, 1994; Johnson 1994; Low 1988; Littlemore 2001b; Deignan *et al* 1997: 523), aiming to stress the importance of metaphor in language teaching and learning. Metaphorical competence is believed to be a competence both for native speakers and foreign language learners. It is regarded to be more important for advanced learners if they are to attain a level of language proficiency in, for example, English, that will equip them for professional lives that require a high level of language awareness, knowledge, understanding and resourcefulness (Bailey 2003: 6). Danesi (1994: 462), in studying metaphor research and the teaching of Italian (native language), emphasizes the importance of metaphor learning for native Italians, saying that "to ignore metaphor is to ignore a large segment of the (Italian) native-speaker's competence". And he (1986: 9) also points out that "the ability to 'metaphorize' in a second language is the true sign that the learner has developed L2 communicative competence", because if people were limited to strictly literal language, communication would be severely curtailed, if not terminated (Johnson 1994: 456). Ponterotto (1994) holds a similar view that "one of the many problems in the teaching and learning of a foreign language is the acquisition of competence in the area of figurative language", believing that the ability to grasp metaphorical expressions is considered to be characteristic of advanced stages of language competence.

However, metaphor is omnipresent in language and

metaphorical language is hard not only for native speakers but also for foreign language learners (Cooper 1999; Bennett 1994; Buchwald 2000; Wu 2003; Boers 2003). In exploring foreign language learners' problems in understanding English university lectures, Littlemore (2001c: 338) shows that over 90% of areas of difficulty could be described as metaphorical. Danesi (1994: 453-458) points out that learners, even after several years of study, have not mastered metaphorical language, which results in unnaturalness in their speech. Danesi suggests that the main reason is not that learners are incapable of learning metaphor, but more likely that they have never been exposed in formal ways to the conceptual system of the target language and culture. Difficult as it is, teachers and learners must be prepared to meet the challenge. Rare but not come singly, Johnson (1996: 237), a prominent figure in cognitive linguistics, considerably strengthens the previous idea, claiming that figurative language[1] should be the primary focus of L2 learning, and that teachers and materials should not avoid metaphor in early learning.

Nevertheless, in practice, metaphor has not been given sufficient attention in the field of language teaching and learning, FLTL field in particular, for some reasons or other. One of the reasons the present research comes to be aware of is concerned with most language teaching practitioners' inadequate understanding of the nature of metaphor[2]. This is because metaphor has long been viewed, along the traditional line, as a purely linguistic phenomenon, which is regarded as just being nice and ornamental in nature, with its cognitive orientation and foundation unknown or neglected. Possibly for this reason and the difficulty of summarizing the connotative meanings of words, "Most textbooks skirt the issue of figurativeness and concentrate on the denotative aspects of language. Although some idiomatic phrases are usually included in first-level coursebooks, they are usually presented as exceptions to the rule, things to be learned very often as fixed expressions and to be used in specific contextual situations. In later phases, work on figurativeness is suggested through reading and vocabulary building exercises, and students are often referred to specialized learner dictionaries of idioms, phrasal verbs, etc.. It is common that intensive work on the figurative use of language is left to courses on literature, and metaphor especially is tackled through the presentation of literary texts" (Ponterotto 1994). This is the general situation of metaphor teaching and learning worldwide.

The previously discussed phenomenon, i.e., lack of knowledge of relevant theory on the part of language teachers, is not uncommon for foreign language teaching and learning and it is even more difficult and challenging to avert its direction in Chinese context, due to its unique features and the status quo of the practitioners (Yang 1999: 420-427). To fully clarify it, we will delineate briefly the current situation of Chinese foreign language teachers. More specifically, and generally, there are three sorts of attitude among Chinese teaching practitioners towards importance and utilization of relevant theories in classroom teaching. Firstly, influenced by traditional views, many, if not all, Chinese teaching practitioners are neglectful and oblivious of the role and necessity of the relevant theories in language teaching practice. Foreign language teaching is often seen as an activity only involving "mouth and ear", a technique requiring no theoretical guidance. Rather it is a craftsmanship which needs only artistic skills. Opposite to this fact is a dogged and relentless pursuit of any new breakthroughs in theory and a timely and blind adoption of them. In fact, this characterizes language teaching worldwide, because "The field of language teaching is always keen on developing the pedagogical implications of theoretical linguistics" (White 2003: 147). Admittedly, however, many, if not all, of these followers are deficient in distinguishing the merits and demerits of different schools of theories and the applicability of them in language teaching context. They blindly believe in and adhere to paradigm shifts and scientific revolutions in the field (Yang 1999). These blind followers, as American scientist Kuhn describes with a metaphor, tend to use the new paradigm like a foreigner in an unfamiliar land, forever struggling with the new categories, new terms, materials, theories and shifts in significance, since they find that a new model seems simpler, more elegant, or more attractive than the old (Willis & Willis 2002: 8)[3]. Thirdly, there are also some practitioners who, for some known reasons of their working reality, on the one hand, believe in the usefulness of relevant theories, and on the other, feel at loss as to how to specifically operationalize them in classroom teaching practice. In other words, what they lack is the concrete and effective techniques that can be used in classroom teaching. This general situation is even truer of metaphor teaching in foreign languages.

Consequently, the central, perhaps thorny problems for foreign language teaching research, particularly metaphor research, for the time being are correspondingly three-folded. Firstly, practitioners should arrive at an adequate and deep understanding of the relevant theories, thus making an appropriate use of them in classroom teaching. Specifically, for metaphor teaching in particular, they should broaden their knowledge about the different kinds of metaphor theory, at least acquire some knowledge about Aristotle and Lakoff's metaphor theories since the two, as will be discussed in the next chapter, are the most influential. Secondly, practitioners should be well aware of the real nature of foreign language teaching (FLT). As a discipline with special features, FLT is currently considered to be strongly influenced by eclecticism (Yang 1999). Therefore, it is suggested that contributions from other fields such as philosophy, psychology, linguistics and possibly cognitive sciences as well can be eclectically and integratively adopted to facilitate teaching instead of favoring one at the cost of another (Block 2001; Cook & Seidlhofer 2000: 7). In addition, foreign language teaching is contemporarily believed to be more like a theory consumer rather than a theory creator, and no dramatic and paradigm shifts or revolutions are unlikely to take place (ibid.), so researchers and practitioners are not expected to spare no efforts to create absolutely new theory as a guidance. To sum up, the selection and application of theories should, to the present researcher, be conducted to cater for the philosophy and the intrinsic features of foreign language teaching. Thirdly, practitioners are currently expected to devote time and energy to generating effective techniques for classroom teaching rather than developing theories.

Therefore, it seems urgent currently for metaphor practitioners to be well equipped with a theoretical knowledge of metaphor, which can suitably guide real teaching practice effectively. The present research ventures to take it as one of its principal tasks. In other words, it will first try, based on a review of the two most influential theories by Aristotle and Lakoff & Johnson, to give a working definition of metaphor for applied linguistic study, hoping it will benefit metaphor teaching and learning with English as a foreign language. A caveat of the theoretical framework adopted in this research seems quite necessary before the actual analysis.

1.3 The theoretical framework: A caveat

It is widely acceptable that a scientific research is more likely to bear fruit if it is well supported by a proper theory. It is also true of a metaphor study from a perspective of teaching with English as a foreign language (EFL). Unfortunately, however, it is a widespread belief that to do a theoretical work on metaphor is by no means an easy job (Searle 1998: 101; Murphy 1996: 175). When one gets ready, as comprehensively and thoroughly as possible, to reveal the ins and outs of this initially seemingly simple and often-taken-for-granted linguistic phenomenon, he might well be lost in a maze and consequently feels at a loss as to where to get started and which theory about it he should follow. This is because what he faces now is a kaleidoscope of metaphor theories generated in the fields such as philosophy, psychology, linguistics, sociology, to name just a few. As Gibbs (2001: 29-30) points out, the voluminous publications will intimate scholars from taking the plunge into the murky waters of metaphor research.

Precisely knowing the difficulty of doing research in metaphor from a theoretical approach, the present study, to divorce from the possible pitfalls, intends to address the issue from a practical and pedagogical perspective. In other words, its interest lies in finding out which theory, or theories, among others can be effectively used to guide metaphor study in EFL field, since such a theory is urgently needed after a close examination of the relevant literature about FLTL study.

As is demonstrated in the previous sections, a plethora of metaphor theories have to date been presented from different perspectives. It is impossible and inadvisable for the present researcher to make a meticulous analysis of each theory and then to come up with one that is effective at studying metaphor in

FLTL research. Therefore, this research will confine itself to the two most influential theories in history: the classical metaphor theory represented by Aristotle and the contemporary one by Lakoff & Johnson (henceforth Lakoff for convenience), leaving the others untouched as far as possible unless they will have to be mentioned in passing. Aristotle and Lakoff are chosen mainly for two reasons. One is concerned with their prominent and unique, and more importantly, hardly comparable positions they two have occupied in the history of metaphor research. Their views are considered to be more powerful and representative than others. Their respective unparalleled contributions to metaphor study are expressly laid bare in the forthcoming statement.

> "In the beginning there was Aristotle. Then there were the Dark Ages, which lasted until 1980. And then there was Lakoff. There was a Johnson too. But the historian who is after sweeping statements has to be selective. So first it's Aristotle, then Lakoff".
>
> (Steen 2000: 261)

The other is that metaphor teaching in both native and foreign languages so far have followed mainly the theoretical lines established by them, as is discussed in the reviews of many researches.

1.4 Purposes of this research

The questions addressed in this research are based on the results of the comparative study of Aristotle and Lakoff & Johnson' definitions of metaphor as well as Richards' (1965) idea about metaphor as are discussed in the chapter that follows. Specifically, metaphor is cognitive in nature and everyone is capable of dealing with metaphor. If this conclusion is acceptable, then it is assumed that one's ability to deal with metaphor is mainly decided by his cognitive ability and/or metacognitive ability. Of course, the research do not deny the roles played by other factors such as motivation, learning style, age, sex, family background, etc. (Hu 2004: 11). What this research wants to emphasize is that among the many factors that affect metaphor comprehension and production, cognitive ability might be a primary one for the sake of its cognitive nature. Naturally, it can be assumed that native speakers are very likely to differ from foreign language learners in comprehending and producing metaphors. This is believed to be true because generally speaking native speakers are no longer dogged by language problems and are quite familiar with the culture where they live. However, things might be somewhat different for foreign language learners because of their relatively lower level of linguistic competence in the target language. It is assumed that language proficiency[4], besides cognitive ability, might be another primary and important factor that affects foreign language learners' metaphor comprehension and production. In addition, it is believed that cognitive ability and language proficiency might play different roles in the two processes when learners, foreign learners in particular, are at different levels of cognition and language proficiency. Accordingly, the present research intends to examine the following questions.

1) Are Chinese EFL learners' metaphor comprehension and production cognitive or linguistic tasks or both? That is, are Chinese EFL learner's cognitive ability and language proficiency significantly related to their English metaphor comprehension and production?

2) How do Chinese EFL learners' cognitive ability and

language proficiency affect their metaphor comprehension and production when they are at different cognition and language proficiency levels?

3) How do Chinese EFL learners' cognitive ability and language proficiency affect their comprehension of each of the four types of metaphorical sentence and affect their performances with respect to the aptness, novelty and density of the metaphor produced?

4) To what extent do Chinese EFL learners with varying degrees of cognitive and linguistic ability differ in their comprehension of the four types of metaphorical sentence and differ with respect to the density, aptness and novelty of the metaphor generated?

1.5 Terminological issues

1.5.1 Conceptualization of cognitive ability

As is stated in the above section, the present research is mainly concerned about the roles of cognitive ability and language proficiency in the Chinese EFL learners' metaphor comprehension and production, and it is, therefore, quite necessary to define the two terms first. Cognitive ability is a frequently used term in cognitive sciences. Although different definitions are given in different sciences to meet different aims, it is generally considered to be any cognitive activity that is associated with enhanced cognitive processing. Specifically, it is regarded as a conscious intellectual activity such as thinking, reasoning, remembering, imaging, or learning words. For the present research, Gyori's theory seems to be more revealing. Gyori (2002: 128) relates cognition and language, believing that cognitive processes operate in the minds of individual speakers accompanying their current linguistic behavior. Based on this theory, the present research refers to cognitive ability as the ability that learners possess to know the world, i.e., the ability to find the differences and similarities between the things they intend to know, and the ability to make use of their linguistic knowledge to express them, and the ability to know the world with the help of their linguistic knowledge. More importantly, it also refers to learners' awareness of dealing with the above-mentioned things. In other words, cognitive ability defined here also includes learners' metacognitive ability. Metacognition[5] is included mainly for the reason that relevant studies show that it usually overlaps with cognition because the same strategy can be cognitive and metacognitive as well (Livingston 1997; Collins *et al* 2006: 1) and that it closely interacts with cognition, although some researchers distinguish one from another[6] (Sjostrom 1998: 72; Graham 1997: 42-43). Flavell uses an example to show how metacognition interacts with cognition, which is illustrated in the following.

> For instance, we suddenly get the vague sensation (metacognitive experience) that we may not fully understand what we have just read, so we review (cognitive action) the material and our interpretation of it in order to find out exactly what, if anything, is amiss (another metacognitive experience). Or we may decide to read something for some purpose (establish a goal) and start by skimming parts of it (cognitive action) in order to get some initial sense of how hard the going is likely to be (metacognitive experience).
>
> (Forrest-Pressley & Waller 1984: 1)

Therefore, the two strategies are closely intertwined and

dependent upon each other, any attempt to examine one without the other would not provide an adequate picture (Livingston 2006: 3). Since cognition and metacognition run concurrently in the process of a cognitive activity, it can be inferred that learners who are cognitively competent should be those who are metacognitively competent. With this inference in mind, the present research conceptualizes cognitive ability as an ability to be both cognitive and metacognitive.

1.5.2 Conceptualization of language proficiency

As is discussed the previous section that cognition and language is closely related to each other and linguistic ability is also an important part of cognitive ability because people often use their linguistic knowledge to express the differences and similarities that they find about the world and to know the world around them. This seems to suggest that there is no need to distinguish between linguistic ability and cognitive ability. However, things might be different, at least to some extent, for people of different language proficiency levels. In other words, the linguistic ability for L1 speakers and L2 speakers, especially those with a low degree of L2 proficiency, might play different roles in their cognitive processes of the world. L2 speakers, due to their relatively low degree of proficiency in their foreign or second languages, often seek recourse to their L1 knowledge in the processes of knowing and expressing their ideas about the world, i.e., they express their ideas in L2 and think in L1. This is especially true when foreign language learners deal with abstract or difficult problems. Accordingly, for L2 learners, especially those who are not fully proficient in their L2, their ability to use L2 linguistic knowledge to cognize the world should be doubted, at least, limited. This hypothesis has been confirmed by a series of studies conducted by Jiang (2002; 2004a; 2004b) and Wang & Wen (2002). What is more, even if this relationship is not confirmed from the perspective of second language study, the relationship between language and thought as a philosophical issue is generally debatable. Accordingly, a distinction between cognitive ability and language proficiency (linguistic ability) is reasonable and needed in a research like the present one which aims to look into the respective roles played by each in EFL learners' metaphor comprehension and production.

The definition of language proficiency in second language acquisition research varies considerably due to its complexity and different purposes of relevant researches. Accordingly, no clear agreement on its construct has yet been reached. Generally speaking, however, these definitions can be classified into two types, i.e., language proficiency in the broad sense and in the narrow sense. In the narrow sense, language proficiency is defined to include only some of the linguistic components. For example, some research (Cumming 1989) defined second language proficiency as second language learners' speaking ability. Lee & Shallert (1997) used L2 vocabulary and grammar knowledge as the criterion to measure his subjects' language proficiency, which are considered to be "the clearest examples to represent language proficiency" in L2 reading (Yamashita 2002: 83). In the broad sense, language proficiency is termed as a multi-dimensional concept that comprises components of competencies and skills (Ma 2004: 50). According to Ma (2004), "the competence components are subdivided into comprehension competencies of vocabulary, grammar and discourse and production competencies of vocabulary, grammar and discourse while the skills comprise comprehension skills of listening and reading and production skills of speaking. For instance, Martinez, Jr. (2003) has used the bilingual subjects' general knowledge or ability as their language proficiency to explore the relationship between language proficiency and metaphor processing. As a matter of fact, this broad definition of language proficiency appears to gain in popularity for language itself is complex. Just as Stern (1983: 357) argued that "it would seem more reasonable to assume that proficiency in a language is multifaceted and can best be grasped by identifying two or more components rather than to expect to be expressed in a single concept". Accordingly, language proficiency in the present research is also broadly defined.

1.6 The organization of the book

This book contains six chapters. Chapter 1 is a general introduction, providing a rough picture of the current situation of metaphor research in applied linguistics as well as some relevant terms such as cognitive ability, language proficiency, metaphor comprehension and production. Chapter 2 focuses on the working definition of metaphor based on a comparative study of the classical and contemporary metaphor theories by Aristotle and Lakoff respectively, with a view to advancing a theoretical framework which can be effectively used in applied linguistics. Relationships among metaphor, cognition and language learning are also discussed in this chapter. Chapter 3 is the relatively detailed literature review of metaphor research and, more importantly, problems with it in foreign language (FL) and/or second language (SL) settings[7]. Chapter 4 is devoted to the experiment design in which issues such as subjects, procedures, data collection, scoring are accounted for. Chapter 5 deals with the results and the preliminary discussions of the results. Included in the last chapter are the general discussions, conclusions, implications, limitations of the present research and the suggestions for the future research.

Notes

1. Relevant literature reveals that researchers interested in metaphor study often use different terms to refer to the language that is not literal. The frequently used ones are figurative language, metaphorical language, non-literal language, etc.. As a matter of fact, these terms are often used interchangeably. Therefore, this convention also applies to this study for the convenience of expression.

2. The present author once carried out very informal interviews with most of his colleagues teaching English as a foreign language for Chinese college students, asking them what metaphor is. The result demonstrates that almost over ninety five percent of them responded very without any hesitation that metaphor is a figure of speech; it is rhetorical. When pressed further by questions such as whether they know how to make students master this kind of language phenomenon, many of them gave a negative answer nearly unanimously and acknowledged that they themselves were poorly equipped with this knowledge.

3. Kuhn is a world renown American scientist famous for his book *The Structure of Scientific Revolutions*, first published in 1960, and reprinted for several times. Its publication has stirred a great sensation and restless discussion in different academic circles, among which language teaching is one. Interested readers can refer to Yang Yonglin (1999: 420-427) and Willis &

Willis (2002: 4-9) for detailed information.

4. In this book, language proficiency, linguistic ability, linguistic competence can be used interchangeably to refer to the same thing unless they are emphasized respectively.

5. The study of metacognition can be traced back to Plato and Aristotle when they discuss learners' thinking about their own thinking (Brown 1987). Although they do not ostensibly use metacognition as a formal term, it means almost the same as what the term currently conveys. Metacognition, a term for the concept of thinking about or controlling one's own thinking and learning processes, was not formally introduced until 1976 by Flavell. Flavell (1976: 232) defines metacognition as "one's knowledge concerning one's own cognitive processes and products or anything related to them". It also includes "the active monitoring and consequent regulation and orchestration of these processes in relation to the cognitive objects or data on which they bear, usually in the service of some concrete goal or objective".

6. Graham (1997: 42-43) argues, "The distinctions between cognitive and metacognitive strategies are important, partly because they give some indication of which strategies are the most crucial in determining the effectiveness of learning. It seems that metacognitive strategies, that allow students to plan, control, and evaluate their learning, have the most central role to play in this respect, rather than those that merely maximize interaction and input... Thus the ability to choose and evaluate one's strategies is of central importance." As the definitions of metacognition and cognition suggest, the

defining criterion to distinguish one from the other should be the function each performs in learning or cognitive processes. Accordingly, cognitive strategies are mainly used to help a learner to fulfill a particular cognitive objective while metacognitive strategies are used to ensure that the objective has been met.

7. Applied linguists use a variety of terms such as first language (L1), second language (L2 or SL), foreign language (FL) to differentiate languages acquired or learnt in different contexts. Detailed knowledge of the distinction between these terms can be found in Stern (1997). In the present research, in order to keep the term as consistent as far as possible, we prefer to use foreign language (FL) to refer to the language taught and learnt in a foreign environment, namely, learnt without much contact or communication with native speakers. In other words, it mainly refers to the language besides mother tongue learnt in formal classroom teaching. However, for the sake of convenience and authenticity, we have to follow different terms in description since the terms vary in different literature.

Chapter 2 A Theoretical Framework for This Study

2.1 Introduction

Metaphor can be studied in many different ways and at many different levels (Sternberg *et al* 1998: 277). As this research is principally applied linguistics oriented, it confines itself mainly to the study at the practical level. In other words, it will not examine the strengths and weaknesses of the existing metaphor theories as is followed by many other studies (Searle 1998; Murphy 1996: 173-204). Rather, it will try to reveal the real nature of metaphor based on a comparative analysis of Aristotle's and Lakoff & Johnson's theories, aiming to throw some light on the implications their theories have on language, especially foreign language learning and teaching research and practice and thus provides a theoretical framework for the present study.

2.2 The classical theory of metaphor

There is a general consensus among the researchers in metaphor study that "any serious study of metaphor is almost obliged to start with the works of Aristotle" (Ortony 1998: 3). Aristotle's theory is generally regarded as the classical one. His discussion of the issue, principally in his two erudite works: *Poetics* and *Rhetoric*, has remained influential to this day (ibid). For some self-evident reasons, these two monumental works have been handed down from generation to generation mainly in the form of versions of translation and commentary (Harris & Taylor

1989: 20-34; Halliwell 1987; Golden & Hardison 1989; Kennedy 1991; Grube 1958). Naturally, the corollary turns out to be that these translated versions have become the main sources of the subsequent overwhelming majority of criticisms of Aristotle's remarks on metaphor. Admittedly, the present research does not make an exception in this line.

A reading of these translated versions manifests that the central idea of Aristotle's metaphor is found in his two relatively authoritative and extraordinarily influential statements. To well understand Aristotle's main idea about metaphor, we quote them in full as follows.

> "Metaphor consists in giving the thing a name that belongs to something else; the transference being either from genus to species, or from species to genus, or from species to species, or on grounds of analogy. That from genus to species is exemplified in 'Here stands my ship'; for lying at anchor is the 'standing' of a particular kind of thing. That from species to genus in 'Truly ten thousand good deeds has Ulysses wrought', where 'ten thousand', which is a particular large number, is put in place of the generic 'a large number'. That from species to species in 'Drawing the life with the bronze', and in 'severing with the enduring bronze'; where the poet uses 'draw' in the sense of 'sever' and 'sever' in that of 'draw', both words meaning to 'take away' something. That from analogy is possible whenever there are four terms so related that the second is to the first as the fourth to the third; for one may then metaphorically substitute the fourth for the second or the second for the fourth. Now and then, too, they qualify the metaphor by adding on to it that to which the word it supplants is

> relative. Thus a cup is in relation to Dionysius what a shield is to Ares. The cup accordingly will be metaphorically described as the 'shield of Dionysius', and the shield as the 'cup of Ares'. Or to take another instance: As old age is to life, so is evening to day. One will accordingly describe evening as the 'old age of the day'—or by the Empedoclean equivalent; and old age as the 'evening' or 'sunset of life'. It may be that some of the terms thus related have no special name of their own, but for all that they will be metaphorically described in just the same way. Thus to cast forth seed-corn is called 'sowing'; but to cast forth its flame, as said of the sun, has no special name. This nameless act, however, stands in just the same relation to its object, sunlight, as sowing to the seed-corn. Hence the expression in the poem, "sowing around a god-created flame". There is also another form of qualified metaphor. Having given the thing the alien name, one may by a negative addition deny of it one of the attributes naturally associated with its new name. An instance of this would be to call the shield not 'the cup of Ares', as in the former case, but a 'cup that holds no wine'".
>
> (*Poetics* 21 from Harris & Taylor 1989: 31-32)

Clearly, Aristotle does three things in this lengthy and often-cited quotation, which offers us a general picture of his notion of metaphor. First, he defines metaphor as "giving the thing a name that belongs to something else," it is the "transference of a term from one thing to another." Second, he considers that this transference is realized in four channels, namely, "from genus to species, or from species to genus, or from species to species, or on grounds of analogy." To Aristotle, the transference can be made between different entities, i.e., things from different domains. Lastly, Aristotle throws light on the two qualifications for a metaphor to be a metaphor. According to him, a metaphor is qualified by "adding on to it that to which the word it supplants is relative"; and another form of a qualified metaphor is one that, when having been given the thing the alien name, it may, by a negative addition, be denied "one of the attributes naturally associated with its new name". To put in Black's words, "The negation of any metaphorical statement can itself be a metaphorical statement" (Ortony 1998: 34).

In addition to the preceding frequently quoted remark, another, probably the most influential account of metaphor ever provided, is Aristotle's brief and insightful statement as follows,

> "It is a great matter to observe propriety in these several modes of expression—compound words, strange (or rare) words, and so forth. But the greatest thing by far is to have a command of metaphor. This alone cannot be imparted to another; it is the mark of genius, for to make good metaphors implies an eye for resemblances." (*Poetics* 22 from Cameron & Low 2001: 72; Kittay 1989: 2; Hu 2002: 178)

In this brief statement, Aristotle emphasizes the importance of using "unusual words" with propriety for creating the best writing style. And it is in this context that he touches upon the relationship between metaphor and genius.

The two previously quoted statements give a clear and panoramic picture of Aristotle's view of metaphor, which have evoked a veritable plethora of comments and conjectures from many, if not all, metaphor theorists. They believe that Aristotle views metaphor as primarily decorative and ornamental in nature. It is not necessary; it is just nice (Glucksberg 1989: 126). More eye-catching is the nonconstructionists' view that metaphor is unimportant, deviant, and parasitic on "normal" usage (Ortony 1998: 2). Viewed as such, metaphor is called a figure of speech, and its study is confined to literature and rhetoric. The word "metaphor" is thus defined as a novel or poetic linguistic expression where one or more words for a concept are used outside of their normal conventional meaning to express a "similar" concept (Mahon 2001: 72; Yu 1998: 1; Ortony 1998: 202).

The working mechanism and understanding of metaphor has never ceased to catch researchers' attention. Theoretical studies since Aristotle to the present, according to Searle, can be roughly divided into two types: the comparison view and the semantic interaction view (Martinich 1990: 413; Ortony 1998: 3). Aristotle's *Rhetoric* is generally quoted as the source of the comparison view of metaphor, as well as of the view that the topic and vehicle of a metaphor may belong to the same category. Contemporary theorists share this general view and treat comparison as the basic process underlying metaphor comprehension (Glucksberg & Keysar 1998: 422). Theorists constantly voice their viewpoints of Aristotle's theory. For example, Richards claims that, in addition to the topic and the vehicle, Aristotle's notion of metaphor contains another element: the grounds. The original idea or context is the topic, the borrowed idea or notion is the vehicle and the shared element, the grounds (Ortony 1998: 3). For example, in a metaphor such as life is a lottery, *life* is the topic, *lottery* is the vehicle, and the grounds are: *we don't know what the outcome will be* (Charteris-Black 2000: 151; see also Murphy 1996: 175). The comparison view of metaphor is often illustrated this way. When we say A is B we mean that "A is like B in certain respects"; in this view, the hearer tries to perceive something in common between two superficially different entities through establishing analogy between them. In this respect, the comparison view sees metaphor as condensed simile and interpretation as requiring identification of what the topic and vehicle have in common (ibid.).

This sketchy coverage of Aristotle's views of metaphor will serve as a source of the counterevidence for the widespread and arbitrary belief that his notion of metaphor is purely linguistic on the one hand, and the justification for his cognitive consideration of metaphor on the other. Before discussing the cognitive concern of Aristotle's metaphor, let's first look at what metaphor is in cognitive linguistics, i.e., the contemporary theory of metaphor. This is necessary because the contemporary metaphor theory is widely hailed as in direct opposition to the classical theory.

2.3 The contemporary theory of metaphor

The contemporary theory of metaphor is derived from and is a very important part of cognitive linguistics. It is, therefore, necessary to make a brief introduction to cognitive linguistics before a detailed description of the contemporary theory of metaphor is made. In addition, a discussion about the relationship between cognition and metaphor needs clarification.

2.3.1 Introduction to cognitive linguistics

Cognitive linguistics is defined as "an approach to language that is based on our experience of the world and the way we perceive and conceptualize it" (Ungerer & Schmid 2001: F36). Philosophically, cognitive linguistics rests on experientialism as its theoretical foundation. Experientialism emphasizes the role of human body in the formation of concepts, and one of its central notions is embodiment, which means that thought and understanding are characterized in terms of our having our particular kind of bodies (Rakova 2004: 19). A basic assumption of the philosophy is that language is closely related to human experience; that human experience with the world, to a great extent, determines language structure and meaning (Wang & Li 2004: 1). Based on this assumption, cognitive linguists believe that knowledge grows out of human experience of the world and, in turn, "our shared experience of the world is also stored in our everyday language and can thus be gleaned from the way we express our ideas" (Ungerer & Schmid 2003: F38); and meaning is characterized in terms of embodiment, that is, in terms of our collective biological capacities and our physical and social experiences as beings functioning in our environment. Human bodily experience is assigned a central role in meaning, understanding, and reasoning (Yu 1998: 22). What is worth noting here is that experience should not be understood here as only physical experience with the world. Other human experience such as the nature of our bodies, our genetically inherited capacities, our modes of physical functioning in the world, our social organizations, etc., are also included (Lan 2003: 28).

Cognitive linguistics is a branch of linguistics that approaches language from the perspective of cognition. Therefore, to study metaphor in cognitive linguistics, we have to first of all explicate what cognition is and its relationship to metaphor.

2.3.2 Relationship of cognition and metaphor in cognitive linguistics

Cognition is etymologically originated from the Latin word *cognitio* meaning the action or faculty of knowing or learning, which is one of the three important domains in psychology research (Zhao 2002: 1). With the rise and development of cognitive science, the nature of the term seems to appeal to more researchers. Cognition in cognitive sciences is generally defined as the exercise of human intelligence, and it is believed to be essential to everything we do (Osherson 2000: xi). Specifically, it is a mental process or mental construction connected with understanding, formulation of beliefs, and acquisition of knowledge as well as expression for intention and attitude to knowledge, etc. (Sjostrom 1998: 72; Ortony 1998: 1; Kittay 1989: 9). Cognitive linguistics, as a branch of cognitive sciences, assumes that "in the relationship between language and the physical or objective world there exists an intermediate level 'cognition'" (Lan 2003: 22; Svorou 1994: 4). Thus, language is viewed as an integral part of human cognition (Langacker 1987: 12). Therefore, language study is an essential part of the study of human cognition and metaphor study constitutes an essential part of cognitive linguistics. And more importantly, as far as linguistics is concerned, an account of linguistic structure should articulate with what is known about cognitive processing in general (Langacker 1987: 12). Since, in cognitive linguistics, metaphor is primarily viewed as a human cognitive mechanism, and since communication is based on metaphor, language is considered as linguistic realizations of metaphor and thus an important source of evidence for what metaphor is like. Therefore, the importance of metaphor to language and cognition cannot be over emphasized (Yu 1998: 1). The importance of metaphor study to cognitive linguistics is as metaphor to language and cognition. Just as what Hamilton (2004: 104) points out, "It is fair to ask where cognitive linguistics would be today without metaphor. Without its enquiry into metaphor, this relatively young branch of linguistics might have been slower to transform the tree to which it belongs, then now seems evident".

2.3.3 Metaphor: A contemporary view

The field of metaphor studies has appealed to a growing number of researchers, at least partly due to the fact that there is a strong realization that metaphors are part and parcel of everyday life (Sardinha 2002: 1). In the cognitive paradigm into metaphor research so far, Lakoff & Johnson have emerged as true pioneers with their seminal book *Metaphors We Live By* published in 1980 (Cameron & Low 1999: 77; Yu 1998: 2). What follows will be a brief introduction to metaphor in the cognitive paradigm largely based on Lakoff & Johnson's ideas.

The contemporary theory of metaphor maintains that human conceptual systems are to a large extent metaphorical in the sense that they contain mappings of inference patterns from typically more concrete domains to typically more abstract domains (Yu 2003: 22). Lakoff & Johnson, in their landmark book, strongly believe that "our ordinary conceptual system, in terms of which we both think and act, is fundamentally metaphorical in nature" (Lakoff & Johnson 1980: 3). Interestingly, Lakoff & Johnson make use of a metaphor to give a vivid definition to metaphor in the Afterword to *Metaphors We Live By*, "It is as though the ability to comprehend experience through metaphor were a sense, like seeing, touching or hearing, with metaphors providing the only ways to perceive and experience much of the world. Metaphor is as much a part of our functioning as our sense of touch, and as precious" (ibid: 239). Besides, they emphasize another important feature, i.e., the ubiquity of metaphor, saying that "metaphor is pervasive in everyday life, not just in language but in thought and action" (Lakoff & Johnson 1980: 3).

This conception of metaphor is thus thought to be revolutionary against the classical metaphor theory. Lakoff summarizes the qualities of the nature of metaphor in cognitive sense into six aspects, which are quoted in the following.

> 1) Metaphor is the main mechanism through which we comprehend abstract concepts and perform abstract reasoning; 2) Much subject matter, from the most mundane to the most abstruse scientific theories, can only be comprehended via metaphor; 3) Metaphor is fundamentally conceptual, not linguistic, in nature; 4) Metaphorical language is a surface manifestation of conceptual metaphor; 5) Though much of our conceptual system is metaphorical, a significant part of it is non-metaphorical. Metaphorical understanding is grounded in non-metaphorical understanding; 6) Metaphor allows us to understand a relatively abstract or inherently unstructured subject matter in terms of a more concrete, or at least more highly structured subject matter.
>
> (Lakoff 1994: 244)

It can be seen clearly from this quotation that Lakoff attaches great importance to the cognitive feature of metaphor. In other words, the fundamental role that metaphor plays in comprehending abstract concepts and in performing abstract reasoning. And we also notice that, Lakoff, in this statement, acknowledges that much, rather than all subject matters, is to be understood through metaphor. It thus implies that the world can be understood non-metaphorically and metaphor is only one of the mechanisms by which people use to know the world.

2.3.4 Conceptual vs. linguistic metaphors

In cognitive linguistics, metaphor is termed as a human

cognitive mechanism by which human beings know the world around them. It is fundamental to the structuring of our thought and language, and that we frequently use the concepts and lexis from one semantic area to think and talk about other areas (Deignan, Gabrys and Solska 1997: 352). What crucially concerns us here and the key to understanding metaphor from a cognitive-linguistic perspective are the distinction between conceptual metaphor and linguistic metaphor advanced by Lakoff and Johnson. The term "conceptual metaphor" is used to refer to a connection between two semantic areas at the level of thought, while the term "linguistic metaphors" are the spoken or written realizations of a conceptual metaphor. Within the cognitive approach to metaphor, primacy is given to the conceptual rather than the linguistic level of metaphor analysis. Lakoff & Johnson shed some light on this distinction when they elaborate on why a concept is metaphorical and how it structures everyday activity. Specifically, in the case of the concept ARGUMENT[1], it is generally, at least in English culture, viewed in terms of the conceptual metaphor represented in the upper case as ARGUMENT IS WAR. This conceptual metaphor is reflected in English language by a wide variety of expressions, which are what they term as linguistic metaphors:

ARGUMENT IS WAR
Your claims are *indefensible*.
He *attacked every weak point* in my argument.
His criticisms were *right on target*.
I *demolished* his argument.
I've never *won* an argument with him.
You disagree? Okay, *shoot*!
If you use that *strategy*, he'll *wipe you out*.

He *shot down* all of my arguments.

(Lakoff & Johnson 1980: 4)

According to Lakoff & Johnson, people understand "argument", a more abstract domain, by way of their concept or knowledge of "war", a more concrete domain. That is to say, underlying the understanding of their conceptual knowledge of argument is their knowledge of or experience with war. With this clear example, Lakoff & Johnson remarks, "It is in this sense that the ARGUMENT IS WAR metaphor is one we live by in this culture; it structures the actions we perform in arguing" (ibid.). Lakoff & Johnson also argues that people usually argue or reason following typically certain patterns because people of a culture generally share the same or similar concepts which systematically influence what they do, think and say. Cognitive linguists hold that conceptual metaphors are mostly unconscious, operating beneath the level of cognitive awareness as part of mechanisms of thought (Lakoff & Johnson 1980: 5; 1999). However, they are always there functioning, and are accessed on occasions where need arises to guide one's reasoning and use of novel metaphorical expressions (Yu 2003: 28). Linguistically, Lakoff & Johnson claim that the conceptual metaphor is realized by the linguistic metaphors, namely, the italicized linguistic expressions, as shown in the above example. Meanwhile, they further claim that linguistic usages frequently reflect our inherent metaphorical understanding of many basic areas of our lives (Lakoff & Johnson 1980; Sweetser 2003: 17). This leads Lakoff & Johnson to reason that: metaphor is not in the words, it is in the ideas; it is part of ordinary language, not only of poetry; it is used for reasoning. Meaning is in the mind, not in the world (Scaruffi 2006: 4). The two linguists also point out something that is more enlightening to language teaching and learning, i.e., the language people use to talk about the aspect of the concept is systematic because the metaphorical concept people live by is systematic (ibid, 7). Rephrasingly, besides the systematicity found in the reasoning of abstract concepts, there is also a systematicity in the usage of conventional expressions and novel language constructions. And this systematicity of the expressions in turn implies that many of these expressions have a common metaphorical derivation (McGlone 1996: 545; Sweetser 1990). In other words, linguistic expressions are therefore ultimately grounded in experience: bodily, physical, social and cultural (Popova 2003: 139).

So far we have accounted for the notion of metaphor in cognitive linguistics. It can be seen that the basic features of metaphor in the cognitive linguistics discussed previously can be summarized into four points. Firstly, metaphor is a cognitive tool by which people comprehend abstract concepts and perform abstract reasoning. Secondly, metaphor is pervasive in everyday activities. Thirdly, metaphorical language is just linguistic realizations of conceptual metaphors. Lastly, since conceptual metaphor is systematic in nature, the language that reflects it is also systematic.

2.4 A critical analysis of the classical theory of metaphor

2.4.1 Introduction

This section is intended to, based on what are discussed in sections 2.2 and 2.3, work on the real nature of metaphor in Aristotle's theory. To elucidate the nature, the section will first make an attempt to reveal the cognitive foundation of Aristotle's metaphor, the possible reasons for the misunderstanding of his metaphor theory, the similarities and differences between the classical and contemporary metaphor theories. The section concludes with a new understanding of Aristotle's metaphor.

2.4.2 The classical theory of metaphor: a cognitive perspective

2.4.2.1 Introduction

Aristotle's theory of metaphor is widely and traditionally viewed as purely linguistically-oriented, especially with the birth and development of cognitive linguistics in 1980s (Kittay 1989: 4; Mahon 2001: 72). His metaphor theory is often greeted with a prevailing negative appraisal (Mahon 2001: 69), for someone believes that "It is with Aristotle's famous definition that the troubled life of metaphor begins" (Johnson 1981: 5).

Provided in the following are the two currently representative and authoritative criticisms against Aristotle's metaphor theory from Lakoff and Johnson, two influential pioneers of cognitive linguistics. In the introduction to his monumental piece *The Contemporary Theory of metaphor*, Lakoff (1998: 202) points out, "In the classical theories of language metaphor was seen as a matter of language, not thought. Metaphorical expressions were assumed to be mutually exclusive with the realm of ordinary everyday language: everyday language had no metaphor, and metaphor used mechanisms outside the realm of everyday conventional language." Johnson (1981: 5-6) holds that Aristotle's metaphor is limited in various ways. First, metaphor is restricted to the level of word, rather than the sentence. Secondly, metaphor is viewed as deviant from normal usage. Thirdly, metaphor is considered to be based on similarities between things. The previous criticisms, however, to the present research, sound too extreme because they are not a faithful and comprehensive reflection of Aristotle's notion of metaphor. The following section will be devoted to unveiling Aristotle's concern over the cognitive importance of metaphor based on a careful and close scrutiny of the two frequently quoted statements. Certainly, our analysis will be conducted from the aspects which the contemporary cognitive metaphor theorists claim that Aristotle's metaphor does not hold.

2.4.2.2 A Cognitive foundation of Aristotle's metaphor theory

As was mentioned previously, Aristotle's view of metaphor has been often greeted with negative appraisal especially with the rise and prevalence of cognitive linguistics largely because some relevant studies insist that Aristotle undervalues metaphor and believes it to be merely an ornamental extra in language (Mahon 2001: 69), which means that Aristotle is thought to have neglected the cognitive importance of metaphor. However, recently some analytic philosophers have redressed an injustice for Aristotle. As is known, metaphor is not just a subject matter of linguists, the study of it has also been a major concern of philosophers throughout history. What kindles the author's interest is the analytic philosophers' viewpoint of the nature of metaphor. Specifically, there appears a most pronounced fervour for metaphor among analytic philosophers who make attempted reconciliation and compensation for centuries of neglect. In other words, these philosophers study metaphor not for its affective and rhetorical efficacy, but for its cognitive contribution. They argue that "if metaphor is to be prized, it must do work, and the work that most interests philosophers is that which is cognitively meaningful", and that "Aristotle has already pointed out the cognitive importance of metaphor, particularly metaphor based on analogy" (Kittay 1989: 2).

Firmly guided and strongly encouraged by the idea in the analytic philosophy, the following part will attempt to perform an in-depth analysis of metaphor, hoping to reveal its cognitive feature. And this analysis will be based on the two currently influential statements about metaphor by Aristotle as are indicated in section 2.2 and the criticisms from theorists of the contemporary metaphor.

The first statement is generally considered to be a definition of metaphor given by Aristotle in *Poetics*. For the sake of convenience, we quote it briefly here again. To Aristotle, "metaphor consists in giving the thing a name that belongs to something else; the transference being either from genus to species, or from species to genus, or from species to species, or on grounds of analogy" (*Poetics* 21 from Harris & Taylor 1989: 31-32).

Admittedly, this definition, if taken entirely literally, conveys nothing of cognitive feature of metaphor for the reason that the comparison or transference is made directly between the names of two things, linguistically, between two nouns. However, if taken non-literally, it will throw light on Aristotle's cognitive concern of metaphor. It is common sense that names or nouns are labels or symbols for the things. On the surface, what Aristotle compares is two names or nouns. However, if we get into the whys and wherefores of the matter, we would surely become puzzled at the comparison. Then a question would arise of why Aristotle took pains to compare the two names or nouns. Is he merely interested in the similarity between the pronunciations and/or spellings of these names or nouns? The answer is certainly negative. Naturally, it is safe for us to believe that Aristotle can not go so far as to do so. Likewise, if we go one step further, we can find that what Aristotle compared is in fact the features, intrinsic or extrinsic, of the things suggested by the names or nouns. The comparison is conducted for the purpose of understanding one kind of thing by way of another. For example, when we say *Mr. Smith is*

Aristotle, it is clear that we compare Mr. Smith to Aristotle in order to know what Mr. Smith is like. And it is also clear that what we compare here are not the pronunciations and/or spellings of the two names or nouns, *Smith* and *Aristotle*. Instead, we compare certain characteristics of the two figures such as their scope of knowledge, their personality, their intelligence, or their influences on the world depending on the context where the sentence is uttered. More importantly, when we make the comparison, as Richards claims (Ortony 1998: 3), we should first of all perceive that there are some shared elements (the grounds) between *Smith* (the topic) and *Aristotle* (the vehicle) (Charteris-Black 2000: 151; see also Murphy 1996: 175). This perception of the shared elements between these two superficially different entities (here *Smith* and *Aristotle*) undoubtedly involves the use of our cognition. Besides, based on our already existing knowledge, we know that the vehicle *Aristotle* is noted remarkably for his broad and profound knowledge. In Giora's (1997; 1999) words, generally, this most salient feature of *Aristotle*, i.e., knowledgeable or critical in thinking, is thus transferred to *Smith*. Therefore, by comparing *Smith* to *Aristotle*, we get to know clearly what *Smith* is like. Just as Anderson said in 1964, linguistic metaphors involve the application of word or expression that properly belongs to one context to express meaning in a different context because of some real or implied similarity in the referents involved (Paivio & Walsh 1998: 309). It goes without saying that it is unlikely for Aristotle to compare the linguistic or semiotic symbols, i.e., names or nouns. Thus it can be seen that this comparison or transference involves a projection of knowledge in one domain onto another, which is very similar to the view of the contemporary metaphor theory as was discussed previously.

Another word that catches our eyes in Aristotle's definition of metaphor is analogy (emphasized by analytical philosophers), which can also be taken as a justification for Aristotle's concern of cognitive orientation in metaphor. Then, what is analogy in Aristotle's definition of metaphor? What does Aristotle mean by "on the grounds of analogy"? More importantly, is his analogy different from what it is held today? Certainly, no one can say *yes* to this question. To better know what analogy is, let's look at how it is defined in different disciplines. Analogy is defined in philosophy as likeness or similarity, usually with the implication that the likeness in question is systematic or structural. To argue by analogy is to infer from the fact that one thing is in some respects similar to another and that the two things will also correspond in other, as yet unexamined respects. In logic, reasoning by analogy is a form of non-demonstrative argument which, unlike INDUCTION proper, draws conclusions about the nature of a single unknown thing from information about a known thing or things which it to some extent resembles (Bullock & Trombley 1999: 27). Cognitive psychologists point out that analogy is one of the most basic cognitive mechanisms of the human mind. People make sense of the world by recognizing similarities, i.e., by noticing that certain new experiences are similar to old ones in specific ways (Gyori 2002: 137). Holyoak & Thagard (1997: 36) argue that the analogy has a certain purpose, i.e., it is guided by what the reasoner intends to achieve by it. More interestingly and convincingly, Lakoff (1998: 235), in his classic work, *The contemporary theory of metaphor*, opens up a special part describing analogy, arguing that it is also a kind of mapping between two cognitive domains in which metaphorical mechanism is also used. In discussing the coincidence of language and reality, Kittay (1989) indirectly points out the function of analogy, saying that discerning analogical uses of language can help us to discern analogical states of reality. Analogy with a cognitive importance is clarified by an example given by Aristotle in defining metaphor. He chose the phrase "sowing around a god-created flame" (*Poetics* 21 from Harris & Taylor 1989: 31-32.) as an example. According to Aristotle, the casting forth of seed-corn, is called sowing, but the act of the sun casting forth its flames has no special name. This nameless act, however, stands in just the same relation to its object, sunlight, as sowing to the seed-corn. Therefore, through an analogical transfer of meaning, this nameless act gets its name similar to the sowing of seed-corn. This example implies that metaphor is itself instrumental in having identified something to be named. It thereby provides us with a way of learning something new about the world, or about how the world may be perceived and understood (Kittay 1989: 2-3). Based on these preceding statements about analogy, we can safely conclude that Aristotle viewed analogy as important for reasoning because he most valued metaphor based on analogy (Kittay 1989: 3). Just as Bowdler & Gentner (1999) assert, metaphor can be seen as a species of analogy. Accordingly, as analogy is a kind of cognitive mechanism, metaphor, as a species of it and as a comparison based on it (Aristotle) is undoubtedly cognitive by nature.

Having discussed about the cognitive concern of Aristotle's metaphor based on his first statement, we will now move on to his second one, which is given in his *Poetics* 22. It is known that Aristotle made this statement in discussing about the relationship between using metaphor and genius. Unfortunately this statement has provoked a controversy centering on at least four claims concerning metaphor, which are generally attributed to Aristotle. One of the claims, which are most closely and negatively related to the present research, is that "metaphors have no cognitive value, and are considered to be merely decorative extras" (Mahon 2001: 72). Fortunately, to the present researcher's knowledge, currently, a few, if not many, linguists (Kittay 1989; Mahon 2001) have come to realize and cast light on the cognitive respect of Aristotle's theory, saying that limited understanding and/or misunderstanding stem from "shallow scholarship about rich and important sources of work on metaphor and language use" (Mahon 2001: 69). For example, according to Mahon (2001: 75), misinterpretation of Aristotle's overall position on metaphor results from the ignorance of and lack of familiarity with *the Rhetoric*[2], another important work in which Aristotle discussed metaphor. The present research fully agrees with Kittay and Mahon to their refutation about the unfair treatment to Aristotle, arguing, depending on Aristotle's second statement, that his metaphor is clearly cognition-based. The reason why such a view is held is that Aristotle in his second statement clearly claimed that "to make good metaphor implies an eye for resemblances" (Mahon 2001:72). Apparently, here "an eye for resemblances" is not an eye for the resemblances between the linguistic factors or linguistic features of names or nouns concerned. Instead, they must be some factors or features conveyed or suggested by the things compared. More specifically and clearly, Aristotle viewed a good metaphor as "an intuitive perception of similarity of dissimilars". It is through resemblances that metaphor makes things clear (ibid). Therefore, we have every reason to believe that Aristotle regards metaphor as a cognitive tool by which we perceive the similarities between two different things.

Of course, when we acknowledge that Aristotle's view of metaphor is cognitive, we can not ignore the fact that his second statement about metaphor is somewhat problematic. This is because he considered the ability to command metaphor as something "which cannot be imparted to another, and it is the mark of genius." This is believed to be Aristotle's too extreme and incorrect an interpretation of metaphor. As a matter of fact, using metaphor is not just an ability unique to poets. Rather, just as Richards says, "we all live, and speak, only through our eye for resemblances. Without it we should perish early. Though some men may have better eyes than other, the differences between them are in degree only." (Hu 2002: 178). Richards' idea of metaphor is undoubtedly more real because in our daily conversations we find that people frequently use metaphors, and that they sometimes create novel metaphors. In other words, what they differ is the contexts where metaphors are used or created rather than what metaphor really means.

Now we can see clearly that although Aristotle mainly discussed metaphor in the context of poetry writing and does not apparently and directly claim the cognitive concern of metaphor, it does not necessarily mean that cognition plays no role in his metaphor. In other words, it is believed that although Aristotle attached importance to the esthetical or rhetorical functions of metaphor in order to make what is said or written pleasing, nice, his metaphor is also cognition-based. And it is in this sense that we can say the classical metaphor theory has something in common with the contemporary metaphor theory. Up to now, we can safely conclude that the traditional view of Aristotle's metaphor as purely linguistic and rhetorical is at least to some extent problematic and incomplete. Therefore, we should give a deep bow to Aristotle for having misunderstood him for so long (Kittay 1989: 2). However, when we acknowledge that Aristotle's metaphor is cognition-based, i.e., it is the same as metaphor in the contemporary theory, it does not necessarily mean that there are not any differences between the classical and the contemporary metaphor theories. And these differences will be examined in the next section.

2.4.3 Basic differences between the classical and the contemporary metaphor theory

The preceding section carries out an in-depth analysis of the cognitive foundation of Aristotle's metaphor. The analysis thus reveals that Aristotle's metaphor is to a certain degree similar to that of Lakoff & Johnson in that they both have a cognitive concern. In this section, the differences between the classical and the contemporary metaphor theory are to be discussed. This research, based on the previous discussion, comes to realize that the two theories differ mainly in two aspects. One is that the two theories differ principally in their perspectives on what metaphor is used for, i.e., the aims or purposes in using metaphor. In other words, Aristotle and Lakoff & Johnson approach the matter from different perspectives, or, they focus their attentions on different features or functions of metaphor. Aristotle, due to the reasons given in the previous subsection, undoubtedly and mainly expands on the linguistic or rhetorical functions of metaphor without explicitly touching upon its cognitive importance. Put it alternatively, although Aristotle's metaphor is cognition-based, it is used mainly to achieve rhetorical effect, i. e., to make expression more lucid, pleasing and nice. This is almost a universally acknowledged understanding of Aristotle's metaphor, which deserves no further illustration. Importantly and logically, that Aristotle did not explicitly mention that metaphor is not a matter of thought does not necessarily mean that he views metaphor just as a matter of language, as is said by Lakoff (1998: 202). As a matter of fact, besides emphasizing the rhetorical effects by using metaphor, Aristotle also touches upon implicitly the cognitive end of metaphor because he believes that people actually learn and understand things better through metaphors (Mahon 2001: 70). This might be the possible reason why some people even regard the cognitive metaphor theory is just a reproduction of the classical theory (Rakova 2004: P. 16). Contrastively, Lakoff & Johnson give priority to their attention to the cognitive concern of metaphor with its rhetorical effect unmentioned. Take LOVE IS A JOURNEY metaphor (Lakoff & Johnson 1980) for example. Lakoff and Johnson cite this example in order to show that metaphor is a universal human cognitive mechanism by which people know the abstract concept LOVE by way of using the concrete and familiar concept JOURNEY (Lakoff & Johnson 1980; Yu 1998). It is clear that they place emphasis on the cognitive function of metaphor. Another important difference between the two theories is considered to lie in their views of the distinction between literal and figurative (metaphorical) meaning (Charteris-Black 2002: 106). Generally the classical view holds that there is a fundamental distinction between literal and figurative language. But this view is greeted with a contradictory view from cognitive linguists, who believe that it is hard to draw a clear distinction somewhere between the truly literal and truly figurative (Gibbs 1994). However, for a research from applied linguistics perspective such as the present one, a distinction between literal and metaphorical language seems necessary and important. However, this distinction should not be like what it is held in the classical metaphor theory, namely, it is clear. Rather, the distinction is just a matter of degree. This view is held because without the notion of literal language it would be problematic to identify linguistic or conceptual metaphor. And additionally, as a matter of fact, metaphor lies on a distinction between a source domain in which words have normal or unmarked senses and a target domain in which the same words have less common or marked senses (Charteris-Black 2002: 107).

2.4.4 Possible reasons for the misunderstanding of the classical theory of metaphor

With a relatively thorough analysis of the cognitive foundation of Aristotle's metaphor and the differences between the classical and the contemporary metaphor theories performed, an attempt at uncovering possible reasons for the limited understanding of his metaphor seems causally necessary. It is obvious that the reasons for the limited and incomplete understanding are not sole. The first, probably the most principal one, might be a neglect, or even ignorance of the context in which Aristotle discusses metaphor. It is well-known that any scientific research in a particular period of history can not avoid the influence exerted by the then conditions such as the dominant philosophy, human cognitive ability, scholars' interest, etc.. It is known that in ancient Greece, people were mainly interested in philology, rhetoric, literature, etc., subjects which are closely related to language. More importantly, dominating these academic fields was Plato's Naming Theory (Dai *et al* 1998: 72)[3], whose influence on the other disciplines is enormous. Probably due to these reasons, Aristotle got interested in rhetoric and talked about metaphor by saying that "metaphor consists in giving the thing a name that belongs to something else". There accrues a misunderstanding of his metaphor as a sole comparison between two names or nouns without cognitive importance. The second reason is believed to have something to do with the level of human cognitive ability. Because of limitation of some objective conditions at that time, people in general had a far less knowledge about the world and themselves, especially about their mind, than what they do now. In other words, they were not so sophisticated as to pay close attention to human cognition then. As a matter of fact, cognitive linguistics which views metaphor as human cognitive mechanism is a product of the cognitive sciences which turned up not long ago. Therefore, it is easy to understand that Aristotle did not definitely pronounce the cognitive concern of metaphor. However, his view of metaphor is not unitary as what we imagine. Rather "Aristotle uses the word metaphor in a wider sense than we do, for almost any kind of transference (Gould 2002: 36). It is quite clear now that the contemporary linguistics treats metaphor as a cognitive mechanism because the cognitive sciences, which rose in 1960s and bloom in the recent two decades, shed more light on the nature of human mind. In this sense, cognitive linguists are luckier than Aristotle so as to pronouncedly declare the cognitive concern of metaphor. The third, a relatively more specific reason might be that "we do not have the complete set of the *Poetics*, and also that, as Grube has said, 'More clearly than any other work of Aristotle, the *Poetics* can only have been a set of lecture notes with later additions and interpolations by the lecturer himself.' As a result, there are many lacunae in the text, among them the absence of a passage explaining the term *ornamental* " (Mahon 2001: 70). Due to this fact, Aristotle's definition of metaphor is often studied independent of its proper context. Misinterpretation because of this fact is very likely to crop up.

2.5 A brief conclusion

The preceding sections spare no effort at disclosing the cognitive foundation of Aristotle's metaphor and the differences between the classical and the contemporary metaphor theories. Accordingly, it is safe to conclude that on the one hand metaphor is not purely cognitive as what Lakoff & Johnson (1980) consider it to be; on the other hand it is not merely linguistic or rhetorical as what Aristotle has been understood. Rather, it is fundamentally cognitive and is used to perform both cognitive and linguistic functions.

As is known to us, metaphor in Aristotle is mainly used for the purpose of achieving rhetorical or ornamental effect, i.e., making the expression more vivid and nice. To clarify and justify this claim, let's perform an analysis of the following situation when we want to say someone has a wide scope of knowledge. Generally speaking, there are two kinds of linguistic expressions for the proposition: *He is knowledgeable* and *He is an encyclopedia*. Apparently, the former is often regarded as literal while the latter is thought of as metaphorical. As far as the rhetorical effect is concerned, the metaphorical expression is much more vivid and effective than the literal one. Therefore, the metaphorical expression is said to have achieved its rhetorical effect. This is what Aristotle's metaphor has been traditionally and currently understood to be. Put it another way, metaphor seems to be just a linguistic phenomenon for the sake of achieving rhetorical effect, a purely linguistic phenomenon without a cognitive concern. However, it is strongly argued in this research that cognition involves in this metaphorical expression of the proposition. This is so because when the writer or speaker compares *He* to *encyclopedia*, he must first of all perceive that there must be something in common between these two entities (persons). Put it technically, the writer or speaker compares *he*, the tenor, to *encyclopedia*, the vehicle, because he finds that there is something in common *knowledgeable*, the ground, between the tenor and the vehicle. Naturally, on the contrary, if the writer or speaker is unable to find a vehicle to which the tenor is similar, it is likely that he is to express his idea literally. But generally he is able to do so because human cognition is fundamentally shaped by various processes of figuration (Gibbs 1998: 253). And this working process of finding the commonalities between the two entities apparently needs cognitive efforts on the part of the writer or speaker. Correspondingly, processing (understanding) the metaphorical expressions, as what Grice implies, requires additional cognitive effort on the part of listeners or readers (ibid). And apparently, this working (cognitive) process precedes the process of language expression. In other words, cognition is fundamentally cognitive. This is why it is strongly argued in section 2.5.2 that Aristotle's metaphor is also cognition-based.

Therefore, this research would come up with a tentative conclusion that when metaphor is used to achieve rhetorical and communicative effects, cognition plays a decisive role. Rephrasingly, metaphorical expression requires cognitive effort on the part of the writer or speaker. And it is in this sense that metaphor is considered to be both cognitive and linguistic.

With the previous conclusion arrived at, it seems here and now logically necessary to give a more practical and unified working definition of metaphor for an applied linguistics research as the present one. As is known to us, metaphor in the traditional line is just seen as a figure of speech which is differentiated from simile, metonymy, personification, proverb and idiom involving conceptual mapping, etc., for the reason that they are different in expressive strengths, linguistic realizations or some other respects. However, from the perspective of cognition, they are qualitatively similar to each other in that they all involve a comparison between two entities about their certain appearances, qualities or features, etc.. More specifically, this comparison is a mapping across conceptual domains, the source domain and the target domain, as is described in the contemporary metaphor theory (Lakoff & Johnson 1980). Actually, the two terms here are quite similar to "tenor" and "vehicle" termed by Richards (1965) in discussing the working mechanism of metaphor as is mentioned in section 2.2. This is something in common among these figures of speech. With this similarity here, metaphor in the present research is thus taken as an umbrella term covering all the other figures of speech which involve the conceptual mappings across cognitive domains (Moser 2000).

In addition to its cognitive and rhetorical functions, metaphor is also considered to perform other communicative functions through language besides its cognitive and rhetorical functions. For example, Sticht (1998: 622), in studying metaphor as communication, thinks that metaphor can serve as linguistic tools for overcoming certain cognitive limitations, arguing that metaphor functions as a tool to extend the capacity of active memory using medium of speech in communication. Fainsilber & Ortony (1987: 240-241) make an assumption that metaphor fulfills the necessary communication function of conveying continuous experiential information using a discrete symbol system. And they formulate three hypotheses (inexpressibility, compactness and vividness) whose functions are believed to facilitate learning. The first is that metaphor can make possible the expression of ideas that may be difficult or impossible to express using literal language. This is because certain aspects of natural experience are never encoded in language and metaphor carry with them the extra meanings never encoded in language (Sticht 1998: 622). The sentence "*The thought slipped my mind like a squirrel behind a* tree" is cited as an example to explain that the characteristics of squirrels slipping behind trees (swiftness, suddenness, ungraspableness) are difficult to express using literal language. The second is that metaphor can express ideas compactly in the sense that metaphors help to convey "chunks" of information rather than discrete units. This is so because language partitions the continuity of experience into discrete units comprised of words and phrases having a relatively narrow referential range. The third is that metaphor, perhaps through imagery, can provide a vivid and, therefore, memorable and emotion-arousing representation of perceived experience, which is quite similar to the traditionally held function of metaphor, i.e., achieving rhetorical effect.

2.6 Significance: An applied linguistic perspective

It is a common and interesting phenomenon that in language learning some learners are found to perform better, both in quality and quantity, than others in producing and comprehending metaphors. Take metaphor production for example. When expressing the idea that someone has a wide scope of knowledge, some learners may say literally *He is knowledgeable* while others may express it metaphorically as *He is an encyclopedia*. Actually, in everyday conversations, formal or informal writings, such kind of sentences occurs frequently. Confronted with such a phenomenon, one may naturally ask why some learners prefer to use metaphorical expression while some tend to express it literally.

The present research thinks that the previous conclusion about metaphor throws light on the problem. Since metaphor is fundamentally cognitive, and everyone is capable of dealing with metaphor and they differ only in degree, their cognitive and/or metacognitive abilities[4] might be the most important factors among others such as language proficiency, learning style, motivation, sex, age, etc., which affect their metaphor comprehension and production performances (Brown 1980; Forrest-Pressley & Waller 1984: 3; Li & Munby 1996: 199; Ellis 1994: 546-550; Cooper 1999: 234; Gui 2005: 243-249). Of course, the researcher does not mean to deny the roles played by other factors such as language proficiency, learning style, motivation, etc.. However, things might be different for native language learners and foreign language learners. Generally speaking, native speakers are no longer dogged by language problems, so their ability to comprehend and produce metaphors may be significantly affected by their cognitive and/or metacognitive abilities. Comparatively, for foreign language learners, because of a lower level of linguistic competence in the target language, their language proficiency may be another important factor besides cognitive and/or metacognitive abilities that affect their metaphor comprehension and production performances. Furthermore, it is hypothesized that cognition and/or metacognition and language proficiency play different roles in metaphor comprehension and production because, after all, comprehension and production are two different cognitive processes. Moreover, it is hypothesized that cognitive ability and language proficiency might play different roles in metaphor comprehension and production when learners are cognitively and linguistically different.

Here a heavy stress on the roles of cognition and language proficiency in foreign language learners' metaphor comprehension and production does not mean a denial of the roles of the factors such as learning style, motivation, etc.. Therefore, the present research will conduct an experiment in order to investigate only the roles played by the Chinese EFL learners' cognitive and/or metacognitive abilities in their metaphor comprehension and production. Before doing this, it seems to be necessary to make a review of the relevant studies. And this is the job of the coming chapter.

Notes

1. Cognitive linguists distinguish conceptual metaphor from linguistic metaphor. They think that linguistic metaphors are just the linguistic realizations of the conceptual one. The two kind of metaphor belong to different levels. To clearly show this distinction, they have established a system to mark the two kinds of metaphor. In this system, the conceptual metaphor is represented in capitalized letters such as ARGUMENT IS WAR, LOVE IS A JOURNEY, while the linguistic metaphors are not.

2. It is traditionally believed that metaphor is just a matter of poetry and literature and everyday language has nothing to do with metaphor. And this is also the so-called weakness of the classical metaphor theory attacked by the contemporary metaphor theorists. Actually, in *Rhetoric*, Aristotle clearly points out that metaphor pervades everyday conversations. According to Mahon (2001), one of the reasons for the misunderstanding of Aristotle derives from researchers' unfamiliarity with and ignorance of the relevant statements about metaphor in this works.

3. Naming theory is found in Plato's dialogue *Cratylus*, whose main idea is that the form is a word in a language and the meaning is the object in the world that it stands for or denotes. Words are names or labels for things. In other words, the semantic relationship holding between words and things is the

relationship of naming. This theory dominated the academic field for a very long period of time, but it was later found to be problematic. This is because the view seems to apply only to nouns. However, even with nouns, the theory seems to be weak because it can not account for abstract nouns such as *unicorn*, *fairy*, ghost, etc.. In other words, we can not find physical objects in the world. The theory was thus later replaced by Concept theory (Dai 1998: 72).

4. Metacognitive ability is included here because is considered by most educators to be an element necessary for many cognitive learning tasks (Li & Munby 1996: 1), and a sign of efficient learning in many tasks (Forrest-Pressley & Waller 1984: 2), and a crucial ingredient to successful learning. Besides, on the one hand, cognitive and metacognitive strategies are closely intertwined and dependent upon each other, any attempt to examine one without acknowledging the other would not provide an adequate picture. On the other hand, according to my experience as an English teacher for many years, students seem to differ more in their metacognitive ability in metaphor production. For example, encyclopedia is a word which might be quite familiar to many students, but only a few of them can be expected to be able to produce sentences like "He is an encyclopedia" to mean that someone has a wide scope of knowledge. And when other students hear this sentence, many of them can understand it. This implies that they are able to perceive the similarities between the two items compared. However, these students often fail to produce such kind of sentences. And the present researcher believes this is more likely to be related to their weak metacognitive ability rather than cognitive ability although it is hard to distinguish one from the other.

Chapter 3 A Literature Review of the Relevant Research

3.1 Introduction

This chapter presents an overview of previous studies on the relationships between cognitive ability and language proficiency and metaphor comprehension and production in the perspective of applied linguistics in foreign language teaching and learning contexts. It includes four sections. The first section is a brief introduction to the notion of metaphorical competence in which the principal reasons why metaphor comprehension and production are chosen as a focus of the present research. The second section is concerned about the relevant studies on the relationships between some factors such as cognitive ability, language proficiency and metaphor comprehension and production. The third section deals with some basic issues in applied linguistic studies of metaphor. The fourth section addresses the problems existing in the current metaphor studies in foreign language teaching and learning contexts.

3.2 Metaphoric competence

It is widely accepted that the ultimate aim of foreign language teaching is to cultivate learners' communicative ability. Communicative ability, as is defined by Hymes (1971) using the four questions as a framework, includes both linguistic and pragmatic knowledge (Ellis 1994: 13; Brumfit & Johnson 2001). Since cognitive linguistics highlights the importance as well as the ubiquity of metaphor in language, the ability of foreign language learners to use and understand metaphor begins to drum up the interests of some applied linguists. It is perhaps against this cognitive linguistics background that the concept of "metaphoric competence" was developed.

Proposal and prevalence of the concept of metaphoric competence in language teaching and learning field should be acknowledged as the joint contribution of three influential articles by Danesi (1986), Low (1988) and Littlemore (2001b). Danesi (1986) defines his notion of metaphoric competence as the ability to recognize and use novel metaphors in the course of speaking and writing, which is believed to comprise two aspects: context-appropriateness and instrumental strategy. The former refers to the ability to identify the mental image embedded in the conceptual metaphor while the latter means the ability to rightly use the conceptual schema in communication. Low (1988: 129-134) defines metaphoric competence as mainly consisting of two aspects: awareness of metaphor and strategies for comprehending and creating metaphors. Furthermore, he systematically arranges it into elements as "the ability to construct plausible meanings for there are semantic anomalies and apparent contradictions in utterances", "the ability to differentiate between new metaphors, conventional metaphors and idiosyncratic extensions of old ones." He further suggests developing an awareness of how to avoid the coinage of absurd metaphors and an understanding of the "hedges" which signal whether a statement is to be interpreted metaphorically or not. Last, he argues for the inclusion of the social sensitivity of certain metaphors such as the gender-biased extension of "man" to represent humanity (Holme 2001: 2). It can be seen that his principal aim is to alert learners to the presence and effects of conventional metaphor and pedagogical approaches to achieving this competence in English language teaching contexts. Littlemore (2001b) argues that a speaker is thought to be competent in metaphor if he possesses the following four abilities: ability to create unconventional metaphors, ability to readily understand the polysemous meanings of a metaphor, ability to comprehend original or novel or fresh metaphors, and ability to understand metaphor at ease and speed.

Clearly, the previous definitions of metaphoric competence have something in common. Namely, metaphoric competence can be roughly understood as the competence to correctly recognize, comprehend and use metaphors in communication. In other words, two abilities are generally considered to be quite essential to metaphoric competence: the ability to produce metaphor and the ability to comprehend metaphor. Accordingly, the two abilities come into focus of the present research.

3.3 Factors influencing metaphor comprehension and production

3.3.1 Introduction

It is found that learner factors such as cognitive ability, language proficiency, cognitive style, sex, age, creativity, etc., have effects on metaphor processing. For example, Boers (2000b: 566-567), in discussing the relationship between metaphor awareness and vocabulary retention, pointed out that men and women had different preferences regarding metaphoric themes. According to his study, girls seemed to prefer to talk about the love/friendship in terms of "sharing feelings and secrets" while male students used architectural imagery (love/friendship as a construction that has to be built or can be demolished). Fine &

Lockwood (1986: 147) found that there was a significant sex difference in the production of novel metaphor. High producers of metaphor were significantly more likely to be men and vice versa. Littlemore (2001: 346) found that age might be related to flexibility of metaphor interpretation, i.e., the tendency to find meaning in metaphor decreases with age. Glicksohn *et al* (1993) conducted an empirical research into the relationship between metaphoric thinking and creativity. The result demonstrated that there exists a positive relationship between the two. Fine & Lockwood (1986) have found that learners with high creativity tend to use more metaphors and produce more novel metaphors than those with low creativity in their performance. They have also revealed that learners with flexible cognitive styles use figurative language more effectively and frequently than those with inflexible cognitive styles, and the reverse is also true. As can be seen that the previously discussed studies are exclusively conducted to investigate the relationships of the learner factors to metaphor comprehension and production in foreign language contexts, similar ones are extremely scarce in the Chinese context. Therefore, studies of this kind are definitely needed to investigate the relationships of these learner factors and the Chinese EFL learners' metaphor comprehension and production.

Since the present research is more interested in the roles that cognitive ability and language proficiency play in the Chinese EFL learners' metaphor comprehension and production, the part that follows will focus on the relevant studies that have been found to date. What is worth noting here is that these studies do not use unified terms to refer to cognitive ability and language proficiency. For example, Johnson & Rosano (1993) uses processing capacity for cognitive ability while Martinez (2003) adopts linguistic ability for language proficiency. For the sake of terminological consistency, the present research prefers to use language proficiency throughout the book unless sometimes there is the need to use other terms such as linguistic ability to avoid monotony in expression and inconvenience in direct quotation.

3.3.2 Cognitive ability, language proficiency and metaphor comprehension

The research on the roles that cognitive ability and language proficiency play in metaphor comprehension is comparatively a new area in applied linguistic field. The few relevant studies that have been found so far are those that have been conducted mainly in the recent years and mostly made in English-speaking environments. Reported in detail in the ensuing part are the four relatively influential ones. They are Johnson (1991), Johnson & Rosano (1993), Johnson (1996), Martinez (2003).

Johnson (1991) conducted an experiment aimed at investigating whether there exist differences in the performances in metaphor interpretation by monolingual and bilingual speakers with the contemporary theory of metaphor as the theoretical basis. His monolingual subjects were 34 English-speaking children. The bilingual subjects were Spanish-English speaking children who were divided into two groups according to their stay time in Canada: 21 children who lived in Canada for 3 years or less (which he termed as recent-immigrant group) and 39 children who lived in Canada for more than 5 years (which he terms as long-term resident group). The result showed that these two groups of bilingual subjects performed less well than their monolingual schoolmates on a story-retelling task and a standardized test of oral language proficiency. Two findings emerged from the investigation. On the one hand, no significant difference was found between the long-term Spanish/English group and the monolingual children on level of complexity in metaphor interpretation. On the other hand, the recent bilingual subjects performed less well than the monolingual English subjects on only some of the metaphor items, and even on these items, language group accounted for only 6% of the between-groups variance. Based on these findings, Johnson arrived at a conclusion that proficiency level in L2 had little effect on basic metaphoric mapping process and that processing capability (cognitive ability: mine) and relevant knowledge are the major factors determining complexity level in children's metaphor interpretations.

Johnson & Rosano (1993) investigated the relationships among measures of language proficiency, cognitive style, and metaphor comprehension. In their study, 45 students from a university in Toronto participated in the test, who were divided into three groups of 15. The English speaking group were mostly bilingual while the two English as a second language groups (ESL) resembled each other on relevant demographic variables and differed only in their length of residence in Canada with one living for 2.5 years or less and the other for 3—5 years. All the students were tested in English with the metaphor interpretation task, the picture vocabulary and verbal analogies subscales from the Woodlock Language Proficiency Battery, and the block designs task. The study showed that the three groups were similar in analytical ability and cognitive style and that the English speaking subjects performed at a higher level than the ESL subjects. But the two ESL group were not distinguishable in terms of measured English proficiency. This study seemed to have replicated the pattern found in Johnson (1991). Specifically, though there existed significant differences in language proficiency between the English speaking and the ESL students, the two groups of students did not differ significantly on measures derived from a metaphor interpretation task. Johnson & Rosano thus concluded that linguistic proficiency seems to be unrelated to level of complexity in metaphor interpretation and it is not a barrier to metaphoric communication in second language students. In other words, metaphor interpretation may be more a conceptual than a linguistic task.

Johnson (1996) conducted a similar research to the previously described two experiments using a bicultural developmental design with children of English home background and children of Spanish home background (age groups: 7-8, 9-10, and 11-12). The research was made to examine possible relationships between language proficiency and metaphor comprehension and to compare the size of any language-group effects with the size of effects due to developmental factors such as age and mental capacity. The results turned out to be that age group, and not language group, was the major factor in explaining variation in children' metaphor interpretation.

Different from the above two studies is the research conducted by Martinez (2003) to address the issue how language proficiency may influence the automaticity of non-literal meaning activation. The participants used were mostly English-Spanish bilingual graduates. The Glucksberg 1982 metaphor interference paradigm was used in which the subjects were required to judge the literal truth or falsity of statements of the form *Some Xs are Ys*. The research comprised a series of four experiments. The results indicated that the non-optional activation of the meaning of metaphor sentences is language proficiency-dependent, i.e., language proficiency plays at least some role in determining whether the figurative meanings of metaphor sentences were accessed.

Reported in the above are some of the studies on the relationships of cognitive ability and language proficiency to metaphor comprehension which have been conducted abroad. At home, however, very little research has been found with the exception of Jiang (2006), which was conducted to explore the Chinese speaking English majors' current level of English metaphoric competence. The subjects in his experiment were Chinese EFL learners who were divided according to their year level at university into two groups: the lower-level English major undergraduates and the higher-level English major graduate students. They were administered to 36 close tests provided with metaphorical and non-metaphorical choices. For example, subjects were given sentences like *The mayor will ________ a business delegation to leave for the U.S.A. next month* (NMF: lead MF: head), and they were required to choose one from the two choices (NMF: non-metaphorical; MF: metaphorical). Apart from the major finding that the Chinese EFL learners' metaphoric competence is relatively very low, the research showed that English language proficiency plays a significant role in determining subjects' metaphoric competence. However, this study did not take cognitive ability as a major variable.

3.3.3 Cognitive ability, language proficiency and metaphor production

Metaphor production, as reviewed in section 3.2, is a very essential component of metaphoric competence. Although some researchers lay emphasis on the importance of productive skills for skilled language users (Bailey 2003: 4), relatively little systematic effort has been made to examine metaphor production, as compared with that made to metaphor comprehension (Fainsilber & Ortony 1987: 239). Of the few studies (Fine & Lockwood 1986; Fainsilber & Ortony 1987; Charteris-Black 2002; Danesi 1992; Cortazzi & Jin 2001) that have been conducted to date, all of them are found to be focused on a certain aspect of metaphor production by first or second language learners. For example, Fainsilber & Ortony' (1987) research was about metaphorical uses of language in the expression of emotions. Cortazzi & Jin (2001) explored teachers' and students' metaphor of teaching, learning and language. Unfortunately, none is found to be concerned about the relationships of cognitive ability and language proficiency to metaphor production not only in the first but also in the second language environments. Therefore, it remains to be a promising and interesting field for investigation.

As reviewed previously, no relevant research has yet been found to investigate the roles that cognitive ability and language proficiency play in metaphor production on the part of both native and foreign language learners, however, some basic issues concerning relevant metaphor production need to be carefully considered. Accordingly, this section that follows is going to make a relatively brief review of the studies on the aspects such as methods for metaphor identification, categorization, criteria for measuring novelty, aptness and density—the three component parts by which metaphor production performance is measured.

3.3.4 Basic issues in metaphor production research

3.3.4.1 Methods for metaphor identification

As far as the validity of metaphor research is concerned, the first and foremost important problem is how to identify metaphor, which has, however, never been adequately treated for some reasons or other (Kittay 1989: 40). In recent decades, with the appearance of an increasingly large number of metaphor studies published, researchers have come to realize the importance and difficulty in identifying metaphor. For example, the journal *Language and Literature* edited by Wales (2002) has opened up a special issue comprising four articles discussing the identification procedures. Many other researchers have also contributed to the discussion of this issue (Moser 2000; Caballero 2003; Cameron 2001). Low (2001) makes a comprehensive and comparative analysis of the strengths and weaknesses of each of the currently frequently used procedures, suggesting that one should be careful in choosing the identification procedure and that more importantly a combinative use can prove to be valuable. Low's analysis is closely related to the present research because it is mainly applied linguistics-oriented. Introduced in the following are the three frequently used procedures.

The unilateral identification is the commonest procedure followed by researchers, under which the researcher examines the text and unilaterally decides what is and is not metaphorical. In addition to the two generally held advantages: the relative ease and speed, Low (2001: 49) identifies another two. One is that using the unilateral identification, the researcher can establish the criterion specific to the research project; the other is that the unilateral approach can make it possible for the researcher to be highly responsive to the text being studied and to make use of a wide range of experience from other areas to bear concurrently on the identification decisions. Meanwhile Low (ibid) demonstrates the dangers that may crop up in the process of identifying metaphor by the researcher unilaterally. Firstly, under this approach, the researcher can not avoid problems such as subjectivity or randomness. Secondly, a recency effect is likely to derive from the adoption of this procedure. Put it another way, researchers will be probably influenced by a heightened sensitivity to metaphor with which they have been working in the recent past, which will result in over-identifying or under-identifying metaphors.

The second kind of identification is Think-Aloud proposed by Steen (1994) and Cameron (2001). This method is used to induce the subjects to talk while they perform some task or to make a retrospective verbal report on what they said earlier afterwards. According to Low (2001), although interesting data can be yielded with this method, this form of report can not eliminate all the problems of reactivity, memory and selective reinterpretation. That is to say, subjects may generate reports of their activities which are either tailored to what the researcher wants to find, or which put themselves in a more favorable light.

The third kind is *Post-hoc* technique with which the researcher simply asks the participants what they meant. This technique has the distinct advantage of minimizing researcher bias. Low (ibid) also points out its weaknesses. For example, it would be clearly unlikely to produce helpful results when participants are repeatedly provided with provisional interpretations in order for them to confirm that this is what they probably thought, because sometimes participants do not have a specific meaning in mind and sometimes they just want to be vague or to avoid responsibility. Concomitantly, when asked too aggressively, participants would take evasive actions because they might feel the questioning to be unwelcome. In addition, the *post-hoc* technique is disadvantageous because it might result in a rapid mental overload. Obviously, it is because the questioning has the inevitable effect of increasing information density and the need to ask the participants to make decisions about numerous pieces of very similar linguistic data.

The present research has found other two problems, apart from Low's comments, with the second and the third techniques. Firstly, the two techniques are only suitable for the small-scale investigations with a small number of participants. When a large-scale investigation is performed, many participants are involved.

It is therefore impossible for every participant to report what they think and answer the questions asked. Secondly, even if each participant was given an opportunity to report and answer, the result might be unreliable to some extent. This is because participants may be different in their understanding about the task and its working principle, which may have differential effects on their performances.

The fourth kind is Third Party Judgment. This is a fairly common method used where a transcript is presented to a third party who is uninvolved in the research. Of course, the third party may be one consisting of one or several judges. This method is often adopted because it can eliminate researchers' subjectivity. However, Low (2001: 53) presents us with three problems with the use of it. First, since different people may use different definitions of metaphor, metaphors identified thus may be of different kinds. Second, third parties may want to gloss their decisions using a wide range of terminology. Third, if the third parties are those who happen to have read books on conceptual metaphor, they will very likely identify a larger set of items as metaphoric than do other identifiers.

Because of the limitations of each procedure, Low (2001) suggests a combinative use of the methods. Accordingly, the present research will choose the first—the unilateral procedure, and the fourth—the third party judgment in identifying metaphors produced in the subjects' protocols.

3.3.4.2 Classification of metaphor

Metaphor is complex as far as conceptual domain projections and linguistic realization forms are concerned. From the perspective of conceptual domain projection, metaphor can be classified into three kinds according to the number of projection domains involved. The most frequently encountered is the two domains projection, i.e., the projection is made between two separate entities. Moser (2001: 4) illustrates it with the sentence "*it was completely off limits*" by emphasizing the role of context. According to him, the sentence can be regarded as both metaphorical and non-metaphorical when the context in which it is uttered is not clarified. It is not metaphorical if uttered in the context of a tennis game when "it" here refers to the tennis ball being actually and physically off the limits of the tennis court. This is so because there involves no projection from one cognitive domain onto another. The expression is metaphorical if uttered in the context of an argument or behavior. This is so because there involves a projection from one domain to another. In other words, "*it*" refers to "argument or behavior". Thus, the sentence will turn to "*her argument was completely off limits*" or "*his behavior was completely off limits*". Moser (ibid) explains, "In both cases, inadequate behavior is described in terms of a sports vocabulary, the limits of the playground symbolizing what is still acceptable to the referee who is symbolically represented by the speaker in this example. Tennis play thus serves as an analogy to express the abstract and complex rules of adequate social behavior".

The second is a case where cognitive projection is found between different entities within a single domain as is pointed out by Cameron (2001: 28). A typical example is the relationships of domain projection reflected in metonymy. It can be explained by the relationship between metaphor and metonymy in the traditional sense. According to Gibbs (2001), the two tropes differ in the number of the domains involved. In metaphor (in its traditional sense), there are two conceptual domains and one is understood in terms of another. In metonymy, there is only one conceptual domain, and the mapping or connection between two things is within the same domain. In other words, one entity is used to refer to another that is related to it. Lakoff & Johnson (1980: 35-40) devote an independent chapter to discussing metonymy, saying that "metonymy serves some of the same purposes that metaphor does, and in somewhat the same way, but it allows us to focus more specifically on certain aspects of what is being referred to." It can be seen that Lakoff & Johnson do not treat metaphor and metonymy as two absolutely different kinds of tropes from the perspective of their cognitive function. More sensibly, they should be viewed as differing in degree rather than kind (Walsh 2003: 234).

The third is a case where complex relations among several terms are involved as illustrated by Gibbs (2001: 31). It is sometimes called *xyz* metaphor, which involves complex mappings among several domains (Gibbs 2001: 31; Kittay 189: 289). A large number of proverbial expressions cognitively belong to this kind of mapping. Turner (1991) illustrates it from the perspective of reading, arguing that readers must understand the conjunction between *x* and *z*, which is interpreted in terms of a conceptual domain containing *y*. Take the metaphor **Language is the mirror of the mind** for instance. The understanding of the relationship between **language** and **mind** must be derived from the relationship between **mirror** and **the things** reflected in it. Obviously, this metaphor is more complex.

Linguistically, metaphor is realized in different ways. Traditionally, metaphor is often limited to the level of word, nouns in particular, and the frequently-cited example would be syntactically the nominal form as *A* is *B* or *A* is like *B* (Cameron & Low 1999: 80; 2001). Worse even on the level of word, scant attention has been given to other forms such as verb, adverb, etc.. As far as linguistic forms are concerned, on the one hand, attention should be given not only to the nominal form of metaphor but also to other forms such as verbs, adjectives, adverbs, prepositions, etc.. For instance, a relevant study even finds that verb metaphors occur more frequently than noun metaphors in spoken data (Cameron & Low 1999: 80). As a matter of fact, metaphor can be realized on lexical, sentential and even discoursal basis (Goatly 1997; Chang Zonglin 2002). Take a sentential metaphor for example. The entire sentence *The troops marched on* is used metaphorically when it refers to "children stubbornly refusing to cease some behavior" (Reyna & Kiernan 1995: 310). And the three kinds are, according to (Cameron & Low 1999), given insufficient attention in foreign language teaching and learning.

Due to the complexity of metaphor, therefore, it is advisable that applied linguistics metaphor researchers should give their attention to the different types of metaphor in both cognitive and linguistic senses rather than sacrifice one for the sake of another (Picken 2001: 64).

3.3.4.3 Criteria for measuring density, aptness and novelty

3.3.4.3.1 Introduction

When pursuing a study on metaphor production from an applied linguistics perspective, naturally a researcher has to take into consideration of the issue of how to assess metaphors learners produce. In other words, what criteria does he use to judge whether learners are good metaphor producers or not? This is certainly a critical but difficult issue for researchers because there have not yet been one which is recognized unanimously. It seems, however, that among many criteria, aptness, novelty and density interest researchers most (Boers 2000a; Littlemore 2001a; Reyan & Kiernan 1995; Waggoner, Palermo & Kirsh 1997; Blasko & Briihl 1997; Blasko 1999; Brisard, Frisson and Sandra 2001; Gagne 2002; Danesi 1992).

3.3.4.3.2 Criteria for measuring density

Metaphor is everywhere in the language we use and there is no escape from it. In other words, we are, consciously or not, employing metaphors all the time. It is roughly estimated that a person produces one metaphor every three utterances in everyday conversation (Shu 2003: 1). Therefore, metaphor density should be regarded at least as one of the criteria by which a language learner is judged to be metaphorically competent or not. Unfortunately, however, few studies have been found to give it adequate attention except the one by Danesi (1992: 489-500). Danesi examined how Spanish-speaking learners of English used metaphors in their writings. The result obtained from his research was that the learners demonstrated a high degree of literalness. In other words, the learners seemed to use less metaphors than native speakers in their compositions. However, Danesi did not clearly discuss the method that could be used in measuring metaphor density in foreign language learners' metaphor production. Therefore, criteria for measuring metaphor density are obviously lacking, which should be given adequate attention by applied linguists.

3.3.4.3.3 Criteria for measuring aptness

Aptness is a term used to tell how well a metaphor is judged to be suitable to describe the features of an item to be discussed (McCabe 1988: 106). It is the extent to which the comparison manages to capture the salient properties of the first noun in the comparison. For example, the comparison expressed in a statement such as "*a train is like a worm*" may not be very apt because the comparison between trains and worms does not seem to capture many of the salient properties of trains, such as their strength and power. However a statement such as "*oil is like a liquid gold*" may be very apt because the comparison does seem to capture many of the salient features of the oil, such as its value and rarity (Semino, Heywood & Short 2004: 1277). Generally, the judgment is thought to be complex and difficult because identification of aptness in practice is relative to particular socio-cultural groups and discourse context (Cameron 2001: 103). A commonly used method is one in which native speakers as raters are asked to make the judgment. What should be emphasized here is that the judgment is by no means a simple correctness or erroneousness process. Rather it should be one that is based on the degree of acceptability by native speakers, by which it is meant native speakers tend to react primarily in terms of acceptability versus non-acceptability judgments (Paul 1998). In other words, aptness is a matter of degree, so a clear-cut boundary is fuzzy and hard to draw (Semino, Heywood & Short 2004: 1277). Since aptness is gradable and the boundary is neither clear-cut nor context-free (Cameron & Low 1999: 80), the judgment is often made on a 7-point scale ranging from 1 (nonapt) to 7 (apt) by well-educated native speakers (Blasko 1999; Brisard, Frisson and Sandra 2001; Gagne 2002).

3.3.4.3.4 Criteria for measuring novelty

According to Pollio *et al*'s count, people use 1.80 novel metaphors and 4.08 frozen metaphors per minute of discourse (Glucksberg 1989: 126). Thus, it is estimated that most English speakers utter about 10 million novel metaphors per lifetime (Cooper 1999: 233). This high occurrence or frequency of metaphor use in spoken and written English carry obvious pedagogical implications for learning English as a foreign language in that learners must be prepared to meet the challenge even though complete mastery of them may be nearly impossible (ibid). More importantly, English learners should be well aware that they should not focus their attention solely on those (i.e., frozen metaphors) they come across in their actual learning process. Additionally and hopefully, they are expected to create new (novel) metaphors in order to vividly and effectively express their ideas. Then it goes without saying that metaphor novelty must be a major concern of foreign language teaching and learning research like the present one. With this mind, a researcher has to take into consideration how to judge one metaphor is novel or not. Or in other words, what are novel metaphors? What are frozen metaphors? And what are the criteria for labeling one metaphor as frozen and another as novel?[1]

Generally speaking, most metaphors are not newly created by their users, but all were once novel and new ones arise constantly even in the most common-place of conversations (Paivio & Walsh 1998: 307). Furthermore, as a matter of fact, most novel metaphors are further extentions of the established ones (Boers 2000a: 138). Consequently, it is believed that metaphors fall into two categories: frozen metaphors and novel metaphors. The former are considered to be those metaphors which are commonly used in the language and which are often thought to be treated as single linguistic units by native speakers while the latter are the ones in which ideas compared are combined in new or unusual ways (Littlemore 2001a: 1). However, this obvious distinction is challenged by some researchers (Reyan & Kiernan 1995: 310; Waggoner, Palermo & Kirsh 1997: 220; Blasko & Briihl 1997). They contend that although metaphors are often differentiated into novel and frozen, there should be no absolute criterion by which a metaphor is valued to be frozen or novel. Instead, they believe that metaphors are different in the degree to which they are considered to be novel or frozen. In other words, they suggest that there should be a continuum, ranging from those that are frozen to those that are novel. More related to foreign language learning, what is a frozen metaphor to a native speaker might be a novel metaphor to a foreign language learner when he or she encounters it for the first time (Littlemore 2001a). Therefore, assessment of the novelty of metaphor can not be dichotomous. Accordingly, for the sake of easy operationalization, some researchers (Brisard *et al* 2001; Bowdle & Gentner 1999) have developed a model using a 7-point scale based on adults rating to judge whether a metaphor is novel or frozen. Generally educated native speakers are simply asked to rate the novelty of each metaphor according to the 7-point scale with 1 = very frozen and 7 = very novel. When differences emerge, a third rater is invited to resolve them.

3.3.4.4 Metaphor elicitation

Elicitation is an extremely important procedure in experimental studies because it is concerned about whether the data collected are authentic or intact, which, to a great degree, determines the reliability of the research results. As it is closely related to the present research, a brief discussion about the elicitation problems with the previous relevant studies seems quite necessary.

Generally, three elicitation methods have been used in the relevant studies. Fainsilber & Ortony (1987), in exploring whether certain theme such as emotion description can invoke more use of metaphorical language, used interview as elicitation, during which participants gave oral responses to the experimenter's questions. Specifically participants were asked to bring to mind situations in which they had experienced different emotions. Participants were then required to recall two situations in which they had experienced it, one in which they had experienced the emotion mildly and one in which they had experienced it to an intense degree. Fine & Lockwood (1986) used a modified version of the

Thematic Apperception Test (TAT), which consists of a series of drawings depicting ambiguous situations, as a method to elicit metaphor production. Participants were asked to write short stories about what was happening in each of five pictures. Cortazzi & Jin (2001) conducted an investigation to see how teachers see teaching and learning. Their subjects included both native English speakers and non-native English speakers such as Chinese, Japanese Lebanese and Iranians. They adopted an elicitation method called sentence stem. Subjects were asked to complete a sentence stem like "*Teaching is...*", or "*Language is...*". Learners were encouraged to provide their concepts about the terms given.[2]

3.4 Limitations of the previous research

The findings from the studies reviewed above can be summarized briefly into the following distinct lines. In the first place, cognitive ability has been unanimously found to be a major significant factor which affects the metaphor comprehension of the bilinguals. Secondly, the role of language proficiency in metaphor comprehension has not yet been established. In other words, some studies have found it to be insignificantly associated to the learners' metaphor comprehension while some have demonstrated that it plays a significant role. Therefore, it is still an issue which deserves further investigation.

The findings obtained from the previously discussed studies, though having shed some light to the relationships of cognitive ability and language proficiency to metaphor comprehension, should be generalized with caution for at least some obvious reasons. The first has something to do with the contexts in which language learning and research take place. As is generally known that learners differ enormously in how quickly they learn a foreign or second language, in the type of proficiency they acquire and the ultimate level of proficiency they reach (Ellis 1994: 197). The socio-cultural context can be considered one of important factors with reference to which these differences can be explained. As stated previously, the four most influential studies used either second language learners or bilinguals in countries such as Canada as the participants to investigate the issue. Findings might be different if the research would be conducted in a context such as in China where English is learned as a foreign language. In addition, these studies except Jiang (2006) were conducted between alphabetic or cognate languages such as Spanish and English, which are typologically and culturally more close to each other than to the non-syllabic languages such as Chinese. It is well known that European languages are comparatively similar to each other than languages of other families. In other words, differences between English and other European languages should be smaller than those between English and non-European languages such as Chinese, although some linguists acknowledge universality across languages (Croft 2000). This is especially important to studies on metaphor because it is universally considered to be language and culture-specific. And Jiang (2006), though conducted in a foreign language context, was principally aimed at investigating Chinese EFL learners' metaphoric competence rather than the relationships of cognitive ability and language proficiency to metaphor processing.

The second problem is concerned about the measures used to test the subjects' proficiency with metaphor comprehension. As discussed above, these studies tested subjects' metaphor comprehension by using sentence frames such as "________ is a ________", with either *topics* (my sister or my shirt) or *vehicles* (rock, mirror and butterfly) given for the subjects to choose. This kind of test would be comparatively easier to tackle than the one if subjects were required to understand a complete metaphorical sentence because when the choices were given lucky guess would be more possible to be made. Moreover, the testing materials used in these studies were not classified according to the correspondence or absence of correspondence of linguistic form and conceptual meaning of the items from the target language and source language as what Deignan *et al* (1997) and Charteris-Black (2002) did. This comparative analysis that identifies the types of relationship between figurative expressions in the two languages is considered to measure figurative proficiency more accurately because it includes both differences and similarities in two languages concerned. For detailed information about this comparative analysis, please see the relevant descriptions in the next chapter and Deignan et al (1997) and Chateris-Black (2002).

The third problem is related to the relationship of cognitive level to metaphor comprehension. As stated, many of these studies examined the roles of cognitive ability and language proficiency in metaphor comprehension when the subjects' were divided into different groups according to their language proficiency level. What are the relationships of cognitive ability and language proficiency when learners were at different cognitive level? This is naturally an issue worthy of further investigation.

3.5 A brief summary

The previous part is a brief review of the relevant studies concerning issues which deserve attention in investigating the roles of cognitive ability and language proficiency in foreign language learners' metaphor comprehension and production. The results can be summarized into the following points.

Firstly, cognitive ability and language proficiency have been found to be differently related to metaphor comprehension. Specifically, cognitive ability has been consistently found to be significantly associated with language learners' (mostly bilinguals) metaphor comprehension performances. However, the studies show that the role of language proficiency in metaphor comprehension is still unclear. In other words, some studies have found it to be insignificantly associated to the learners' metaphor comprehension while some have demonstrated that it plays a significant role.

Secondly, the studies on the roles of cognitive ability and language proficiency in metaphor comprehension are found to have some limitations. For example, most studies were conducted in the bilingual contexts rather than in foreign language contexts. Besides, no studies have examined the respective roles of cognitive ability and language proficiency in the comprehension of metaphor when learners are at different level of cognition. Therefore, the findings should be generalized with caution.

Thirdly, the review demonstrates the study on the relationships of cognitive ability and language proficiency to metaphor production is still a field where no researchers have yet set their feet. In addition to this deficiency, the review also discusses some basic issues about which relevant metaphor production studies should be concerned.

Based on the findings obtained from the previous studies, the present research persuasively argues that the relationships of cognitive ability and language proficiency has not yet been settled and thus remains to be a promising issue for further investigation. Such investigations are especially more urgently needed to examine how foreign language learners' cognitive ability and language proficiency affect their metaphor comprehension and production. And the present research will have a go at it in this respect.

Notes

1. Researchers differ in their views about the novelty and conventionality (or frozenness) of metaphor. For example, Littlemore (2001a: 1) thought of frozen metaphors as those metaphors which are commonly used in the language and which are often thought to be treated as single linguistic units by native speakers. Bowdle & Gentner (2001: 91) maintained that frozen or conventional metaphors involve base terms that refer to a literal concept and to an associated metaphoric category. For example, the conventional base term *blueprint* (as in A gene is a blueprint) has two closely related senses: "a blue and white photographic print in showing an architect's plan" and "anything that provides a plan." Conventional base terms are polysemous, and the literal and metaphoric meanings are semantically linked due to their similarity. Conventional metaphors may therefore be interpreted either as comparisons, by matching the target concept with the literal base concept, or as categorizations, by seeing the target concept as a member of the superordinate metaphoric category named by the base term. Littlemore (2001a: 1) contended that novel metaphors are the ones in which ideas compared are combined in new or unusual ways. But according to Bowdle & Gentner (2001: 91), novel metaphor involves base terms that refer to a domain-specific concept, but are not yet associated with a domain-general category. For example, the novel base term *glacier* (as in Science is a glacier) has a literal sense—a large body of ice spreading outward over a land surface—but no related

metaphoric sense (e.g., anything that progresses slowly but steadily). Novel metaphors are therefore interpreted as comparisons, in which the target concept is structurally aligned with the literal base concept. However, metaphoric categories may arise as a byproduct of this comparison process.

2. What should be pointed out here is that the relevant studies reviewed about metaphor production are mostly conducted with native speakers of English as the participants and quite a few take advanced learners of English as a foreign or second language as the subjects such as Cortazzi & Jin (2001) where they are teachers of English who study further in England. These studies are reviewed here mainly for the purpose of making use of the methods that are used because no methods as such are available for a research like the present one which is directed at investigating EFL learners' metaphor production.

Chapter 4 Experiment Design and Data Collection

4.1 Introduction

The discussion in Chapter 2 has led us to believe that Aristotle's view of metaphor is not like what it is traditionally thought to be, namely, it is purely linguistic. Rather, it is considered to be fundamentally cognitive because it is also used by speakers or writers to know one thing in terms of another. Metaphor is thus considered to be both cognitive and linguistic in that cognition plays an important role when speakers or writers employ metaphors in order to make their speech or writing more vivid, persuasive and effective. This is so because when speakers or writers intend to achieve rhetorical effects with metaphors they have to first of all perceive the similarities (internal or external) between the things they compare. In addition, metaphor is no longer believed to be, as what Aristotle held, a unique gift of poet which can not be imparted to another. Instead, as Richards (1965) argues, everyone is believed to possess such kind of an ability, i. e., the ability to make use of metaphor to achieve successful communication, written or spoken. In addition, according to Richards, some men may have better eyes than others, the differences between them are in degree only (Hu 2002: 178). This position on metaphor sounds very much convincing because it comes as a penetrating revelation of the reality of metaphor use in our everyday communication. In other words, it can explain why some people may comprehend and produce more and better metaphors than others.

If such views of metaphor are acceptable, then it will be natural for one to ask what the crucial factors are and how these factors affect language, especially foreign language learners' metaphor comprehension and production. As is discussed in section 2.6, Chapter 2, metaphor comprehension and production are very complex cognitive processes in which many factors such as meta- or cognitive ability, language proficiency, motivation, personality, age, etc., might work simultaneously. Since metaphor is cognitive in nature, learners' cognitive ability might be undoubtedly a deciding factor which affects their metaphor comprehension and production. However, things might be different for native language learners and foreign language learners. As native speakers are comparatively linguistically competent, their ability to comprehend and produce metaphors may be significantly affected by their cognitive and/or metacognitive ability (henceforth: cognitive ability). In contrast, for foreign language learners, because of a lower level of linguistic competence in the target language, their language proficiency may be another determining factor besides cognitive ability that influences their metaphor comprehension and production performances. Furthermore, cognitive ability and language proficiency might play different roles in foreign language learners' metaphor comprehension and production since the two are, after all, two different cognitive processes. Moreover, it is hypothesized that cognitive ability and language proficiency might play different roles in metaphor comprehension and production when learners are at different cognitive and language proficiency levels. Additionally, cognitive ability and language proficiency are believed to be differently related to learners' comprehension of different types of metaphorical sentences and to their performances with respect to the aptness, novelty and density of the metaphors generated.

With these understandings in mind, the present researcher is going to conduct an experimental study to investigate how Chinese EFL learners' cognitive ability and language proficiency affect their metaphor comprehension and production. The research questions are clarified as follows.

1) Are Chinese EFL learners' metaphor comprehension and production cognitive or linguistic tasks or both? That is, are Chinese EFL learner's cognitive ability and language proficiency significantly related to their English metaphor comprehension and production?

2) How do Chinese EFL learners' cognitive ability and language proficiency affect their metaphor comprehension and production when they are at different cognition and language proficiency levels?

3) How do Chinese EFL learners' cognitive ability and language proficiency affect their comprehension of each of the four types of metaphorical sentence and affect their performances with respect to the aptness, novelty and density of the metaphor produced?

4) To what extent do the Chinese EFL learners with varying degrees of cognitive and linguistic ability differ in their comprehension of the four types of metaphorical sentence and differ with respect to the density, aptness and novelty of the metaphor generated?

4.2 Methods and data collection

4.2.1 Subjects

Subjects in this research were eighty nine Chinese speaking students of English drawn from the foreign language department of a technology institute in a metropolitan city of China. Twenty six were male and sixty three were female. These undergraduates were all English majors from four different classes ranging from grade three to grade four, with grade three group consisting of forty eight (F = 35; M = 13), and grade four of forty one (F = 28; M = 13). They were distributed into four classes randomly with each grade having two parallel classes. Their ages ranged from 20 years to 22 years for the third grade subjects and 21 years to 23 years for the fourth grade respectively. What should be made clear here is that although the subjects were from two grades, their college study time span was only half a year. Specifically, the fourth grade subjects entered the institute only half a year earlier than the third grade subjects. Although they varied in time span for college study, they received the same courses offered by the department and were taught almost by the same teachers, of whom the present researcher was one. All of them had studied English for six years in middle school before they entered this institute where the present experiment took place. Most of them had passed Test for English Majors Grade Four (TEM 4), and a small percentage of them had passed Test for English Majors Grade Eight (TEM 8). Emphasis should be laid here that although most of them had passed TEM 4, their scores were relatively lower as compared with those achieved by the English majors of the same grades from other universities[1]. More than ninety percent of them were from city families and relatively financially sound. What should be pointed out here is that these students varied significantly in their academic performances. This variation, on the other hand, provided an objective basis for some comparative studies of relevant issues. In other words, the variation made it theoretically sound for the researcher to carry out certain studies on the Chinese EFL learners' performances of metaphor comprehension and production when they were divided into different cognitive and linguistic groups. Since the experiment was composed of several minor tests and lasted for several days, seven students had not gone through all the tests. Therefore, the data produced by these students were excluded and those by other eighty two students were regarded as valid and used in the analyses.

4.2.2 Materials for the tests

4.2.2.1 Design of cognitive ability and language proficiency tests

4.2.2.1.1 Measurement of cognitive ability

Since the present research is intended to examine the roles of cognitive ability and language proficiency in the Chinese EFL learners' metaphor comprehension and production, relevant to the matter in hand is the measurement of cognitive ability and language proficiency. Generally, researchers differ in their understandings of what cognitive ability is. Therefore, methods used to assess it also vary to a certain extent. Generally used ones are aptitude tests, progressive matrices, short-term memory tests, information processing tests, Kaufman Brief Intelligence Test, and Raven Intelligence Test (Bialystok & Frohlich 1978; Hakuta & Diaz 1985; Chamot & O'Malley 1996; Robinson 2001). These measures are said to have both advantages and disadvantages. Accordingly, the measurement of cognitive ability still remains for further improvement. For this reason the present research intended, for the sake of achieving a relatively high validity, to make use of three tests which were closely focused on testing cognitive ability. The three tests were employed for the purpose of assessing their correlations to the effect of confirming the validity of the cognitive ability measure. Specifically, if the results of these tests were found to be highly correlated to each other, then it would be acceptable and safe to use the scores obtained by the subjects from any of the tests as their cognitive ability measure. And what follows is detailed description of these measures and the respective reasons why they were adopted.

The first one used is the Advanced Raven Intelligence Test (ARIT) developed by British psychologist Raven in 1938. It was adopted by the present research because it was revised by Chinese psychologists from Furen Center for psychology measurement and Consultation of the psychology department of Beijing Normal University and it is the most widely used in Chinese academic fields (Zhang 1989). More importantly, intelligence test scores are often used as a measure of general cognitive ability (source: Wikipedia, the free encyclopedia)[2]. The test is composed of two subtests with the first used as one for familiarizing the testees with how to tackle the questions and the second as a formal test. Altogether, the formal test is made up of 36 questions presented in the form of figure filling. Specifically, each question comprises a big box with nine small figures arranged in regular patterns with the last figure left out. Under the box there are other eight figures from which testees are required to pick one which can neatly fit the pattern of the figures in the box. (Interested readers can refer to appendix I for detailed information.)

The second test used to measure cognitive ability is a creative thinking practice (CTP) designed by the psychologists who revised ARIT mentioned above. This test was used in the present research because on the one hand creativity is undoubtedly one of the important facets of cognitive ability. On the other hand, as was discussed somewhere previously, linguistic ability is also cognitive (the ability to use L1, not that to use L2) and it is covered in this test but not in ARIT. This test is also composed of two subtests with the first used to familiarize testees and the second used in the formal test. CTP is designed to test testees' abilities with fluency, flexibility and originality. It is made up of five tasks. Task one is word association in which testees are given a Chinese character as a starter for them to write out as many words associated with it as possible within certain time. Altogether four characters are given. Task two is to give titles to the stories to be read. The testees are encouraged to give as many titles as they can to the two stories after reading. Task three is about a small design for which the subjects were required to make as many as they can blueprints of a park with seven pavilions that should be connected with paths and the paths and the pavilions should be well arranged for the sake of beauty and convenience for use. Task four is about picture supplementing. Specifically, many ovals were offered for the subjects to create as many pictures as they could with an oval as a part of the picture. Task five is about the drawing of shadow projections of certain objects. Similarly, the subjects were required to draw the possible projections of the objects given. (For more detailed information, refer to Appendix II.)

The third test is a questionnaire which was used chiefly to test the subjects' metacognitive ability because, as was discussed earlier in Chapter 1, cognitive ability in this research was broadly defined as a combination of learners' cognitive ability in its general sense and metacognitive ability, which might be even more important for language learners when dealing with figurative language. According to Collins *et al* (2006:5), among the many methods, the most commonly used to test metacognition so far include self-talk, self-report, and questionnaire. Questionnaire method was adopted in the present research for the sake of easy administration to its large number of participants and transcription convenience. Furthermore, since there is not any standard questionnaire available for the present research to use, the one used in this research was thus designed with reference to the ones by Kasper (1997), Yang & Zhang (2002), Wu & Liu (2004), which were made to examine learners' metacognitive ability in other fields such as reading and writing. The questionnaire was designed based on the 1-5 Likert Scale. Altogether, there were thirty statements and each was followed by five choices for the subjects to judge the degree at which that corresponds the most precisely to their actual fact. For example, a statement would go like this, *I often consciously compare English and Chinese metaphors in order to find their similarities*. Most statements are issued positively with the first choice indicating that it is the most precise and the last one showing that it is the least. Meanwhile some were given negatively with the first indicating that it is the least precise and the last the most precise. The items in the questionnaire were designed to be close-ended for the sake of avoiding ambiguity or uncertainty. Participants were required to choose one from five answers instead of giving their own subjective and/or descriptive answers. To avoid ambiguity and for participants to correctly understand the statements, the researcher described the questionnaire in Chinese. Before the real administration of the questionnaire, the present researcher sought suggestions from some experienced experts in this field. Some of their suggestions were taken into account in the revision of the questionnaire. A pretest had been conducted before the real administration of the questionnaire took place and some modifications were made in order to make it more appropriate. All the above measures were adopted in order to ensure the reliability and validity of the test. Of the three measures, as is known, AIRT and CTP are widely recognized and used by researchers so that their validity is unquestionable. While the questionnaire was designed by the present research only for this experiment, a test had been conducted to assess its validity. After the test, the analysis via the SPSS showed that the internal consistency was 0.835, which proved that the questionnaire was valid (See Appendix III for details).

4.2.2.1.2 Measurement of language proficiency

Language proficiency is a general, sometimes vague, concept. As was discussed in section 1.5.2 of chapter 1, it would seem more reasonable to assume that proficiency in a language is multifaceted and can best be grasped by identifying two or more components rather than to expect to be expressed in a single concept (Stern 1983: 357). Accordingly, language proficiency was broadly defined in this research so as to include learners' competence such as reading, writing, vocabulary, grammar, discourse, etc.. To meet this requirement, the present research decided to take TEM 4 as a test to measure the subjects' English language proficiency. This test was taken because it is generally accepted as a test which is designed to examine the overall competence of Chinese learners who major in English and used by many relevant studies. The test is composed of six parts: writing, dictation, listening comprehension, grammar and vocabulary, reading comprehension and cloze. As can be seen this test includes more than two components, it is thus considered to be suitable for measuring learners' language proficiency.

4.2.2.2 Materials for measuring metaphor comprehension

Metaphor in the traditional rhetoric is regarded as a figure of speech which is differentiated from other figures of speech such as simile, metonymy, personification, proverb and idiom, etc.. However, as is discussed in chapter 2 of this book, it is cognitively the same as those other figures of speech because they all involve a comparison between two or more entities about their certain appearances, qualities or features, or something else concerned, etc.. Accordingly, metaphor in this research is viewed as an umbrella term which covers all the figures of speech provided that there exist projections among two or more cognitive domains. Therefore, materials for metaphor comprehension were collected on the principle that a sentence is regarded as metaphorical if it contains a comparison between two or more entities from different domains. The testing materials were composed of twenty metaphorical sentences which were mostly selected from the book *Metaphor*[3] compiled by Alice Deignan, a well-known applied linguist. The sentences were arranged into four groups based on the extent of conceptual and linguistic correspondence according to Deignan *et al* (1997) model, as was described in Chapter 3. The correspondence is categorized into the following four types: 1) Same conceptual metaphor and equivalent linguistic expression; 2) Same conceptual metaphor but different linguistic expression; 3) Different conceptual metaphors used; 4) Words and expressions with similar literal meanings but different metaphorical meanings. For example, the sentence *As the war progressed, attitudes on both sides hardened* is of the first type because the sense may be taken as equivalent in both English and Chinese since there is a very close correspondence of both linguistic and conceptual content. The sentence "The leader crushed the rebellion with an iron hand" is of the second type because the conceptual content is very close in both English and Chinese but it is conveyed in different linguistic expressions. The sentence *Alison returned, looking sheepish* is of third type because the conceptual content conveyed by the linguistic expressions are different in English and Chinese. The sentence "Mr. Smith had got a bloody nose when he asked his boss for a high pay" is of the fourth type because there is a close correspondence in literal meaning in both English and Chinese but with different metaphorical meanings. Mention should be made here that sentence rather than short text was chosen for the sake of reducing or avoiding the facilitative role that context plays in reading comprehension. That is to say, we just wanted to see which, concept or linguistic correspondence between the target and source languages, is the key to metaphor understanding. To ensure that the selected sentences were the ones which were relatively new to the participants, two teachers who taught the participants from grade one to three Comprehensive English were asked to sort through all the sentences and rejected some sentences which they thought familiar to the participants and added some others which were new (See Appendix IV for details).

4.2.2.3 Materials for measuring metaphor production

As is discussed previously, there is relatively little systematic research on metaphor production. Of the few studies, the materials used to measure subjects' metaphor production are the ones elicited from oral responses to the experimenter's questions (Fainsilber & Ortony 1987), the ones from the Thematic Apperception Test (Fine & Lockwood 1986), and the ones from sentence stem filling (Cortazzi & Jin 2001). It can be seen that the materials collected from oral responses to questions are comparatively not naturally occurring because the subjects are required to state their ideas following the experimenter's way of thinking. The sentence stem filling materials are limited in that the subjects can only produce A is B type metaphor without the opportunity to generate other types of metaphors. To the present researcher, the materials collected from the Thematic Apperception Test are more valid because the subjects can relatively feel free to talk about their views about a certain topic. Therefore, the materials used for measuring the subjects' metaphor production were collected from a modified thematic apperception test. Specifically, different from the method used by Fainsilber & Ortony's method[4], the present research asked its subjects to write out their ideas about a certain theme. In this case, "Love" was chosen. It was chosen because materials for metaphor production should be collected according to the principle that the topics given should be the ones that are very much likely for participants to have to get recourse to metaphor in order to make their ideas clear. More importantly, this topic should be fairly easy for students to express their own ideas without too much constraint (See Appendix V for details).

4.2.3 Testing Procedures

Since the tests were administered among four intact classes and some of them were given simultaneously, the present researcher asked two of his colleagues to invigilate the tests. Before the real tests began, the two colleagues had been trained to familiarize themselves with the testing procedures. All the tests were conducted in the normal classes, which lasted intermittent three days. The subjects were told the real purposes of the tests and were required to take the tests seriously. And they were willing to cooperate with the researcher. Since a series of different tests were conducted, the testing procedures varied from one to another. A detailed explanation of the testing requirements was given prior to the real test until every subject fully understood how to deal with it. Other procedures were described in detail respectively in the following sections.

4.2.3.1 Procedures for the cognitive ability and language proficiency tests

The cognitive ability was measured in the three tests as were described previously in which the subjects were given warming-up exercises before ARIT and CTP were administered for them to familiarize themselves with the tests. They were required to finish ARIT within forty-five minutes and ATP within fifty minutes. The procedure for ARIT was simple which is not described here. Since the ATP was composed of five sections, the time for each section was controlled. In other words, the subjects were not allowed to do the following one before they finished the preceding one within the time allowed. Mention should be made here that for the first two sections (word association and story title supplementing) the subjects were allowed to use the Chinese phonetic alphabets to replace the certain characters they were unable to write. And in doing these two tasks, the subjects were openly encouraged to use their imaginations but not allowed to use dictionaries or any other reference books. It took the subjects about fifteen minutes to finish the questionnaire during which the subjects were required to choose from among the five multiple choices only one that most faithfully reflects their actualities in doing the things described by each statement. The subjects were encouraged to ask for help when they were unable to understand the statement. All the subjects finished the thirty items in the questionnaire.

As far as language proficiency test is concerned, the present research collected the data from the TEM 4, which is a large-scale examination designed and held for English majors once every year with high reliability and validity. Therefore, it is unnecessary to give a detailed description of the procedure here for the time being.

4.2.3.2 Procedures for the metaphor comprehension test

As is shown in section 2.2.3 of this chapter, the metaphor comprehension test is composed of twenty metaphorical sentences which were classified into four types according to the model developed by Deignan *et al* (1997). They were arranged randomly in order to avoid recency effect. All the sentences were printed on a piece of A 4 type paper. The subjects were required to finish reading all the sentences and answer the questions following each sentence. They were encouraged to guess the meaning when they failed to work out the meaning or were not sure at first reading. They were allowed two minutes to read each sentence. Specifically, within the time given, the subjects could reread the sentence for the meaning. But when the time was up, they were not allowed any longer to work on the sentences which they did not comprehend. This was so designed in order for them to finish all the twenty sentences in stead of focusing on any of these sentences with some untouched since, as is described previously, these sentences were divided into four types according to the conceptual and linguistic correspondences between Chinese and English. Because the research was concerned only about whether the subjects understood the sentences or not, they were allowed to write out their answers to the questions either in English or in Chinese when they felt unsafe to express them in English.

4.2.3.3 Procedures for the metaphor production test

As far as metaphor production test was concerned, the subjects were given two pieces of blank paper with the title printed and allowed forty minutes to write in English freely their own ideas and feelings around the topic *love* in no less than two hundred words. The subjects were required to begin and stop writing as soon as they received the orders from the invigilator. They were not allowed to refer to dictionaries or any other reference books for the words unknown to them in the act of writing. However, they could seek help from the invigilator for the words they did not know. This requirement was imposed for fear that the subjects might copy from the dictionary sentences that might be metaphorical. They were told to write as legibly as far as possible. What should be pointed out here is that some subjects' handwritings were extremely illegible so that they were asked to type their handouts after the examination without any change under the supervision of the researcher for the sake of convenience of correction.

4.2.4 Scoring

4.2.4.1 Introduction to scorers

Scoring is a very essential step in the whole research. A scoring system with high reliability can ensure the validity of the test. Several raters were invited and trained in order to achieve this goal, among them three were native English speakers (two men, one woman) with fair college education background and two Chinese professors of English, of whom the present researcher was one, and one graduate student majoring in psychology. The three native English raters were teachers from one Business English Training Centre established in Shanghai. The other Chinese professor of English graduated from a foreign languages university and had taught English in college for nearly twenty years and had an experience of studying in the United States for one year. The graduate student had studied psychology for three years in a psychology department of a normal university in Shanghai. These raters were assigned to different scoring tasks according to the requirements of the tests. Specifically, the three native English speaker raters were engaged in the metaphor production tests with one as a third party judger. That is, when the other two raters differed in their ratings, he was involved to settle the problem. They were involved in these tests because metaphor production is a highly culture-specific activity. Non-native English speakers, even if they are well grounded in English, may not fulfill the job satisfactorily. The other tests were scored by the Chinese professor of English and the present researcher because these tests were not so highly demanding as the metaphor production tests viewed from the perspective of culture.

The ARIT and CTP were evaluated jointly by the graduate student with the present researcher. Other items of secondary importance were done by the researcher himself independently, for example, the scoring of the meta-cognitive ability questionnaire because it was objective. Before the scoring took place, all the scorers had been trained so explicitly that they fully understood the specific requirements of the tests. All the explanations about these items were scored by the raters working independently. Whenever differences arose among the three raters in the scoring of the same item, the present researcher would interpose a discussion in order to reach an agreement. Overall interrater reliability (as measured by simple percentage of agreement, a method adopted by Waggoner, Palermo & Kirsh (1997) is 91.6% among the three English speaking raters and 94.3% among the Chinese professor and the researcher.

4.2.4.2 Scoring of the cognitive ability tests

The cognitive ability test is made up of three subtests, therefore, the scorings of them are described one by one in the following.

Since the ARIT is a sheer objective test, the scoring is relatively easy. Specifically, the subjects' scores were calculated according to the number that they rightly chose. Namely, the more right answers they chose, the higher their scores were. The total score for this test was thirty six.

The scoring of CTP was relatively complex because it was composed of five sections with different requirements. For example, the word association was scored according to the number of the words produced and repeated words were not scored. The total of this section was obtained by the number of correct words multiplied by 0.2. The second section, the story title supplementing, was scored according to the quantity and quality (the degree of the relatedness of the titles given to the stories). Based on the quantity criterion, the scores were derived from the number of the titles given. As far as the quality criterion was concerned, the titles given were classified into three levels according to the degree of their relatedness to the stories. Specifically, those which were considered to be improper or loosely related to or partly summarized the stories were valued 0, and those which pointed out or summarized the main ideas of the stories were valued 1, and those which were profound, original, critical were valued 2. The total of this section was obtained by adding the scores together that the subjects got in the two parts. Some choices were offered for reference on the part of the scorers. Moreover, if the titles that the subjects produced could not be found in the list of choice offered, they would be settled by the two scorers (the graduate student and the present researcher) with a discussion. The third section, a small design for a park, was scored on the quantity and the quality of the blueprints created. By quantity, it was meant that the more blueprints produced, the higher the scores. By quality, it was meant that the seven pavilions should be well connected with the paths rather than positioned in disorder or clustered together without being practical and pleasing to the eyes. In addition, it is better for the paths to link all the seven pavilions together than not. The fourth section, picture supplementing, was scored similarly to section 3, i.e., according to quantity and quality (originality). It was needless to describe the scoring on the criterion of quantity. However, a few words about that on quality seem to be necessary because it is somewhat different from the previous one. The subjects would be given more scores if the pictures created were about the things which were not frequently met. For example, a helicopter would be considered to be more original than a car and a terrestrial globe more original than a cup.

Besides, it was required that the base form, i.e., the oval should be a part of the newly drawn picture. Otherwise, it would be judged to be useless. The last section, the drawing of shadow projection, was scored on the number of the possible correct projections. In other words, those impossible projections would not be included. Altogether, the scores obtained from each section were added up to constitute the total scores the subjects gained in this test[5].

Since the meta-cognitive ability questionnaire (MAQ) was designed on the basis of the 1-5 Likert Scale, the scoring of it was relatively simple. Specifically, scores were calculated according to the number given before each of the five choices. As was stated previously, some statements were issued positively while some negatively. Therefore, the scoring system differs for the two kinds of the statement. Specifically, for the positive statements, when the first choice was circled, it was given a value 5; when the fifth was made, it was given a value 1. A quite opposite scoring system was applied to those negative statements. The points given were added together to form the total score of the subject's performance on the meta-cognitive ability questionnaire.

After the scoring was finished, an analysis was conducted to explore the correlations among the scores obtained from the three tests with the assumption that if significant correlations were found, it would mean that the tests that were used to examine Chinese EFL learners' cognitive ability were valid and reliable because the three tests inter-confirmed each other and accordingly, they, or any of them, could be effectively used in the relevant analyses. To investigate the correlations, a Pearson correlation analysis by SPSS 11.5 was performed. The results indicated that there existed significant correlations among the three tests (ARIT and CTP: $r = .517$, $p = .000$; ARIT and MAQ: $r = .705$, $p =$

.000; MAQ and CTP: $r = .735$, $p = .000$). This means that the scores obtained from the three tests, or that from any of them, can be used as reliable data to reflect the subjects' cognitive ability level. Moreover, it was found that both the scores from ARIT and CTP are nearly equally correlated to that of MAQ, consequently, for the sake of convenience, the score from MAQ was used in the following analyses to investigate the relationships among Chinese EFL learners' cognitive ability, language proficiency and metaphor comprehension and production.

4.2.4.3 Scoring of metaphor comprehension

As was described previously, metaphor comprehension was composed of twenty short metaphorical sentences which were further classified into four types according to the correspondence between English and Chinese in concepts and linguistic expressions. With respect to the comprehension of short metaphorical sentences, a two-dimensional measurement (right or wrong) was adopted to grade the reading comprehension results. If a subject got a correct answer, he would get 1 point; otherwise he would get 0 point. All the points were added up to amount to his total score of this test. Mention should be made here that the subjects' explanations were scored mainly for accuracy of understanding rather than for sophistication of expression in terms of words, grammar, etc.. The total score was one hundred.

4.2.4.4 Scoring of metaphor production

Included in this part are the scorings of the data derived from the topic writing (TW). The two English speaking raters worked together to seek out metaphors in the TW.

Metaphor density analysis was performed on the numbers of metaphor produced in the TW for the purpose of seeing how many metaphors the subjects could produce every one hundred words as was conducted by Fine & Lockwood (1986: 146). Since the subjects varied in length of the topic writings, the points the subjects achieved with respect to density of metaphor were calculated by the following formula:

Density = MN ÷ TNW ×100%

(Here MN is shortened form for metaphor number produced in the writing; TNM stands for total number of words produced in the writing).

Aptness and novelty measurements were done by the two English speaking raters on the metaphors they two had picked out in the TW. And the analysis followed the same procedure. As reviewed above, in L1 studies, a 7-point scale was generally used to measure the degree of novelty and aptness of a certain metaphor as was taken by Blasko & Briihl (1997) and Brisard, Frisson & Sandra (2001). This research, however, challenged the applicability of this method when used in L2 studies. This is because L1 and L2 learners are different from each other in many aspects such as linguistic competence, cultural background, when they are required to write something about an abstract concept. What is implied is that for L2 learners, they might not be so capable of describing their ideas and feelings so minutely as L1 learners. In other words, metaphors produced by L2 learners might not be so exact as to describe the shade of meanings as those by L1 learners. In addition, it is believed that L2 learners might not produce metaphors as frequently as L1 learners. Thus, a too minute gradation might make the statistics too complicated. Accordingly, it seemed unnecessary to make a minute gradation of a metaphor in terms of aptness and novelty. Therefore, a 2-dimensional 5-point ordinal scale was used in this research to measure the two qualities of a metaphor. Each point was given a numerical value according to the degree of aptness and novelty. For example, in measuring aptness of a metaphor, 1 point was given to a metaphor when it was judged to be remotely apt; 2 point when tangentially apt; 3 points when fairly apt; 4 points when apt; 5 points when highly apt. The same measure was performed on novelty of metaphor. For example, if a metaphor was considered by both raters to be frozen, it had the value of 1, somewhat novel with the value of 2, fairly novel with the value of 3, novel with the value of 4, and the most novel with the value of 5. For the sake of clarity, a sentence by one of the subjects would suffice the evaluation. While he described the beauty of his girlfriend, he wrote, "*My love is a rose, she wears a long black hair, has big round eyes, and is very slender*". Here the comparison was made between the loved one and a rose, where the quality of the rose (beauty) was carried over to the live one. In terms of aptness, this metaphor sounds very much acceptable to native English speakers, and consequently it was given a value of 5. However, as far as novelty is concerned, the metaphor is rather frozen because it is widely used by native speakers, and was thus assigned a value of 1.

Particularly emphasized here is that the scores that the subjects achieved on metaphor density, aptness and novelty were transformed into percentile scores in order to make them comparable with those on other tests items such as language proficiency.

Notes

1. The subjects in the present experiment achieved comparatively lower scores in the TEM 4 and very fewer passed TEM 8 with poor results as compared with those by the English majors of the same year levels from other colleges and universities because these students were generally considered to be less intelligent,

motivated and diligent as were measured by the National Matriculation Test, which is held every year as an entrance examination for middle school students to enter colleges and universities.

2. Wikipedia is a very powerful free encyclopedia program covering a wide variety of topics about which people can freely discuss and provide their ideas there for public use and reference. It can be available at: http://www.wikipedia.org.

3. This book is a special bilingual edition with Chinese translations compiled by Alice Deignan and published by HarperCollins Publishers Ltd. and The Commercial Press (Hongkong) Ltd.. The book is arranged according to the theme about the world such as human body, health and illness, animal, and building and architecture, etc.. What is good about the book is that English metaphors are provided with Chinese versions with some necessary modifications made according to the typical features of our Chinese culture. Therefore, it is a useful book for our Chinese researchers and students who are interested in metaphor.

4. Fine & Lockwood (1986) used a modified version of the Thematic Apperception Test to elicit metaphor production. The test is made up of a series of drawings depicting ambiguous situations. The subjects were required to write short stories about what was happing in each of five pictures according to their understanding about what are described by these pictures.

5. This dictionary is a special bilingual edition with Chinese translations compiled by Alice Deignan and published by

HarperCollins Publishers Ltd. and The Commercial Press (Hongkong) Ltd.. The book is arranged according to the theme about the world such as human body, health and illness, animal, and building and architecture, etc.. What is good about the book is that English metaphors are provided with Chinese versions with some necessary modifications made according to the typical features of our Chinese culture. Therefore, it is a useful book for our Chinese researchers and students who are interested in metaphor.

6. As was discussed earlier that the scoring of CTP is relatively complex, what is offered here is only a very brief introduction. Fortunately, the designers of this test supplied us with a scoring direction in great detail. And the scoring was made exactly according to the direction.

Chapter 5 Results and Discussions

5.1 Introduction

The present research was principally concerned about how Chinese EFL learners' cognitive ability and language proficiency affect their metaphor comprehension and production. As was stated in section 1.4 of Chapter 1, the present study focused on four specific questions about this issue. And this chapter would report the results and attempt to have some tentative discussions about them.

It should be pointed out here that the data used in the analyses were collected from a series of tests by using the software package SPSS 11.5. In all the analyses reported below, the level of confidence for rejection of either the alternative or the null hypothesis is .05; actual p values are, however, reported.

5.2 Question 1

Are Chinese EFL learners' metaphor comprehension and production cognitive or linguistic tasks or both? That is, are Chinese EFL learner's cognitive ability and language proficiency significantly related to their English metaphor comprehension and production?

The question addressed in this part is brought up to confirm the hypothesis that was proposed in Chapter 2, namely, the Chinese EFL learners' metaphor learning is neither simply a cognitive process nor simply a linguistic process. Instead, it is both a cognitive and linguistic process. Specifically, it is believed that the success of the Chinese EFL learners' metaphor learning is to a great extent determined by both their levels of cognition and language proficiency in the target language.

5.2.1 Data and analyses

5.2.1.1 Results: metaphor comprehension and cognition and language proficiency

Described below is the descriptive statistics on the scores of the Chinese EFL learners' cognitive ability (COG), language proficiency (LP) and metaphor comprehension ability (MC).

Table 5.1 Descriptive Statistics of the Test Results (COG, LP, MC)

Variable	N	Min	Max	Mean	SD
COG	82	50.00	103.00	77.134	14.768
LP	82	36.00	81.00	66.073	8.482
MC	82	10.00	80.00	52.987	14.160

Note: COG = Cognitive Ability LP = Language Proficiency
MC = Metaphor Comprehension ability

The above table shows that the mean score for the Chinese EFL learners' cognitive ability test is 77.134 (SD=14.768) and for the target language proficiency test it is 66.073 (SD=8.482). The mean score for the metaphor comprehension ability test is 52.987 (SD = 14.160).

Clearly shown in Table 5.1 are the raw data which were normalized separately for each test and, for the statistical purposes, the original scores were transformed into z-scores in order for the tests to be comparable. A Pearson correlation test was run to see the relationships between the Chinese EFL learners' cognitive ability, language proficiency and metaphor comprehension ability. In other words, the correlation test was performed to see if cognition and language proficiency played significant roles in metaphor comprehension ability. As can be seen in the following table (Table 5.2), both the subjects' cognition and language proficiency are significantly correlated to their metaphor comprehension performances (cognition and metaphor comprehension: $r = .701$, $p = .000$; language proficiency and metaphor comprehension: $r = .702$, $p = .000$).

Table 5.2 Correlations of the Three Variables (COG, LP, MC)

Variable (N = 82)		COG	LP	MC
COG	Pearson Correlation	1.000	.603	.701
	Sig (2-tailed)		.000	.000
LP	Pearson Correlation	.603	1.000	.702
	Sig (2-tailed)	.000		.000
MC	Pearson Correlation	.701	.702	1.000
	Sig (2-tailed)	.000	.000	

Note: 1. COG = Cognitive Ability LP = Language Proficiency MC = Metaphor Comprehension Ability

2. Correlation is significant at the 0.01 level (2-tailed).

In order to further investigate whether the two factors, cognition and language proficiency, are significant predictors of metaphor comprehension performances, a multiple regression analysis was conducted with language proficiency and cognition as the independent variables and metaphor comprehension ability as the dependent variable. The result indicates that the two factors account for a significant proportion of the variance of metaphor comprehension ability ($R^2 = .614$, $F = 62.89$, $p = .000$) (see

Table 5.3). It can be seen from the table that both independent factors, i. e., language proficiency and cognition, emerge as significant predictors of the Chinese EFL learners' metaphor comprehension performance. For language proficiency, β=.439, t = 5.01, p =.000, this means that the learners' language proficiency in the test could predict 43.9% of the variation of their metaphor comprehension performance. For cognition, β = .436, t = 4.981, p =.000; this means that the Chinese EFL learners' cognitive ability could predict 43.6% of the variation of their metaphor comprehension performance.

Table 5.3 A Multiple Regression, Metaphor Comprehension Ability as a Function of Cognition and Language Proficiency

Variable	Constant	β	t	R^2	F
COG		.436	4.981		.000 * * *
	−27.72			.614	62.899 * * *
LP		.439	5.013		.000 * * *

Note: COG = level of cognition LP = Language Proficiency MR = Metaphor Comprehension Ability

Df = 2; * * $p < 0.05$; * * * p =.000

Now that both the correlation and regression studies show that the Chinese EFL learners' metaphor comprehension is significantly associated with their cognitive ability and language proficiency, it is necessary to see what kind of relationship that lies between metaphor production process and cognition and language proficiency.

5.2.1.2 Results: metaphor production and cognitive ability and language proficiency

Described below is the descriptive statistics on the Chinese

EFL learners' cognitive ability, language proficiency and metaphor production performances. Mention should be given here that metaphor production in this research is composed of the level of both novelty and aptness.

Table 5.4 Descriptive Statistics of the Test Results

Variable	N	Min	Max	Mean	SD
COG	82	50.00	103.00	77.134	14.768
LP	82	36.00	81.00	66.073	8.482
MP	82	.00	65.75	11.344	12.928

Note: COG = Cognitive Ability LP = Language Proficiency MP = Metaphor Production Performance

The above table shows that the mean score for the Chinese EFL learners' cognitive ability test is 77.134 (SD=14.768) and for the target language proficiency test it is 66.073 (SD=8.482). The mean score for the metaphor production test is 11.344 (SD=12.928).

For the statistical purposes, the raw scores were also transformed into z-scores in order for the tests to be comparable. A Pearson correlation test was performed in order to see whether there exists a correlation between the Chinese EFL learners' cognitive ability, language proficiency and their metaphor production ability. The table below (Table 5.5) indicates the relationship, which demonstrates that both the subjects' cognitive ability and language proficiency play quite significantly positive roles in the Chinese EFL learners' metaphor production performances (cognitive ability and metaphor production performances: r = .769, p =.000; language proficiency and metaphor production performances: r =.395, p =.000).

Table 5.5 Correlations of the Three Variables (COG, LP, MP)

Variable (N = 82)		COG	LP	MP
COG	Pearson Correlation	1.000	.603	.769
	Sig (2-tailed)		.000	.000
LP	Pearson Correlation	.603	1.000	.395
	Sig (2-tailed)	.000		.000
MP	Pearson Correlation	.769	.395	1.000
	Sig (2-tailed)	.000	.000	

Note: 1. COG = Cognitive Ability LP = Language Proficiency MC = Metaphor Comprehension Ability

2. Correlation is significant at the 0.01 level (2-tailed).

Following the pattern that was woven for studying the relationship among cognitive ability, language proficiency and metaphor comprehension performances, the present research conducted a multiple regression test in order to see if the first two variables (cognitive ability and language proficiency) were significant predictors for the Chinese EFL learners' English metaphor production performances using metaphor production performance as the criterion variable and cognitive ability and language proficiency as prediction variables.

The regression analysis, as is shown in the forthcoming table (Table 5.6), accounts for a significant proportion of the variance of the Chinese EFL learners' metaphor production performances (R^2 =.599, F = 59.054, p =.000) (see Table 5.6). However, this result was found to be slightly different from that of what had been revealed about the contributions that cognitive ability and language proficiency have made for metaphor comprehension. Specifically, it is demonstrated that cognitive ability outperforms language proficiency in explaining the proportion of the variance of metaphor production performances. Cognition is apparently found to be still a particularly significant predictor variable in the Chinese EFL learners' metaphor production performances (β= .835, t= 9.347, p=.000). This means that the learners' cognitive ability can predict 83.5% of the variance of their metaphor production performances. On the contrary, language proficiency is shown to be an insignificant variable in the learners' metaphor production performances (β=.108, t=1.215, p= .228). This unexpected result implies that the Chinese EFL learners' language proficiency can only predict 12.15% of the variance of their metaphor production performances.

Table 5.6 A Multiple Regression, Metaphor Production Ability as a Function of Cognitive Ability and Language Proficiency

Variable	Constant	β	t	R^2	F
COG		.835	9.437		.000 * * *
	−34.09			.599	59.054
LP		.108	1.215	.228	

Note: COG = Cognitive Ability LP = Language Proficiency MP = Metaphor Production

Df = 2; * * $p < 0.05$; * * * p =.000

5.2.2 Summary and discussion

5.2.2.1 Summary

The preceding parts are concerned with the relationships that exist among the Chinese EFL learners' cognitive ability, language proficiency and their metaphor comprehension and production performances. The relationships are studied through two kinds of analysis: a correlation analysis and a multiple regression analysis. Findings emerged from the studies can be summarized as follows.

Firstly, in terms of correlation analyses, both the Chinese EFL learners' cognitive ability and target language proficiency are found to be highly significantly and positively correlated with their English metaphor comprehension and production performances.

Secondly, as far as multiple regression analyses are concerned, the results appear to be many-folded. Specifically, it is found that the analyses can explain highly significant proportions of the variance of metaphor comprehension and production performances when cognitive ability and target language proficiency are combined together.

Thirdly, when cognitive and language proficiency are treated separately, different results emerge. In other words, the subjects' cognitive ability and foreign language proficiency are found to be quite significant predictors of the variance of their English metaphor comprehension performances while they are different for metaphor production performances. Namely, cognitive ability appears to consistently predict a significant proportion of the variance of the production performances whereas language proficiency does not.

To sum up, as a whole, cognitive ability and target language proficiency are found to be closely and positively correlated with and to be significant predictors of a proportion of the variance of the Chinese EFL learners' metaphor comprehension and production performances.

5.2.2.2 Discussion

As is summarized in the preceding parts, the results obtained from the relevant analyses, in general, provide evidence in support of the hypothesis that was proposed in Chapter 2, i.e., the Chinese EFL learners' English metaphor learning is both a cognitive and a linguistic process. Namely, it is one in which both cognition and language proficiency are involved. This is so because the correlation analyses demonstrate that both the subjects' cognitive ability and English language proficiency are highly significantly and positively correlated with their English metaphor comprehension and production performances. In other words, the higher the subjects' cognitive ability and target language proficiency levels are, the more competent they are in comprehending and producing English metaphors, and vice versa. The results obtained from the regression analyses further confirm the finding from the correlation analyses because the analysis shows that the Chinese EFL learners' cognitive ability and language proficiency can explain quite a significant proportion of the variance of their metaphor comprehension and production performances. Alternatively, when the learners read and produce metaphorical sentences, their levels of cognition and target language proficiency together determine to a large extent whether they can be successful or not.

It is easy to understand this working process of metaphor learning of foreign language learners. Take metaphor comprehension for example. As is discussed in Chapter 2 and 3, metaphor is fundamentally cognitive and metaphors are mostly created on the basis of the extended meanings of the already existing words and the newly created meanings (metaphorical meanings) of these words are generally culture-specific. Since native speakers grow up in this cultural environment, in the process of living they gradually form certain kinds of habits, concepts or conventions by which they know or conceptualize the world. When they are faced up with the task of knowing one thing (concrete or easy) in terms of another (abstract or difficult), they tend to take relatively similar conceptualizing approaches or methods although there exist some intrapersonal differences. And these are generally deeply rooted in their minds and deeply marked on their language. Consequently, it will be easier or readier for them to understand or work out the similarities or differences between the things compared. More technically, it is easier for them to detect the ground that lies between the tenor and the vehicle. Accordingly, they can make sense of the metaphorical meanings of many of their words or phrases concerned more quickly, effectively and precisely than foreign language learners. As a matter of fact, the metaphorical meanings of some linguistic items are conventionalized or internalized so that native speakers can use and understand them automatically or unconsciously. In other words, when they have acquired their first language, they have acquired the culture conveyed by the language.

For foreign language learners, however, when they learn a foreign language, they often start with learning the basic or denotative meanings of the words or phrases, which are generally the same as those of their first language. Comparatively speaking, many, if not all, foreign language learners are more familiar with the basic (literal or non-metaphorical) meanings of words or phrases than with those metaphorical (non-literal) ones because most textbooks and dictionaries give primary attention to the basic meanings of words and phrases (Ponterotto 1994). Put it another way, foreign language learners have to acquire the literal meaning before they are able to master the metaphorical meanings of words or cultural knowledge. In fact, as Cooper (1999: 233) points out, complete mastery of idioms (metaphorical language) may be nearly impossible. The too loaded task undoubtedly puts them into a distinct disadvantageous position when encountering metaphorical sentences (Cooper 1999: 234). Accordingly, if foreign language learners are not well equipped with the linguistic knowledge of the target language, they need to make much more cognitive effort in order to understand metaphor they meet. What is more, since the conceptual system is L1-based (Kecskes & Cuenca 2005: 51), metaphorical meanings of words or phrases of the target language are most likely accessible only through a process of assimilation and/or accommodation[1] as what Piaget believes (Piaget 1997). If foreign language learners are unable to assimilate or accommodate the metaphorical meanings into their already acquired knowledge scheme, failure or misunderstanding will result. Therefore, mastery of the metaphorical meanings of words and phrases of the target language must be built upon acquisition of the basic meanings of the corresponding words and phrases. And it is in this sense that linguistic knowledge of the target language plays a crucial role in the comprehending of metaphorical sentences. Furthermore, as it is stated immediately above, foreign language learners are relatively more familiar with the basic meanings of target words or phrases, in this situation when they read the metaphorical sentences of the target language, their cognitive ability can compensate for their linguistic deficit if they are cognitively competent. In other words, they can guess the meanings of the words based on the basic meanings because, as is discussed, most metaphorical meanings are derived from the basic meanings of the words. Based on this inference, the results obtained from the preceding analyses in the present research is theoretically and practically sound and acceptable. Consequently, a conclusion can be drawn that metaphor learning for foreign language learners is both cognitive and linguistic.

An interesting phenomenon has been noticed in the process of analysis. That is, although the analyses confirm that the Chinese EFL learners' metaphor learning is both a cognitive and linguistic process, it seems that these two independent variables exert different predictive power on the learners' metaphor comprehension and production performances. As can be seen from the results of the analyses, cognition predicts 43.6% of the variance of the comprehension performances while language proficiency does 43.9%. This seems to suggest that cognitive ability and language proficiency play almost equally important roles in metaphor comprehension. However, the two variables, although when combined together they predict a significant proportion of the variance of the subjects' metaphor production performances, are found to be differentially significant prediction factors when treated separately. The multiple regression analysis shows that cognitive ability turns out to be a significant factor whereas language proficiency does not. This result seems to imply that although language proficiency is significantly correlated with metaphor production performances, cognition appears to be a more important factor determining the metaphor production process. The possible explanation for this phenomenon is that the metaphor production process, unlike metaphor comprehension which often begins with recognizing of linguistic items and then decoding of their meanings especially when insufficient context is given (Gough 1972; LaBerge & Samuels 1974), is concept or thought driven. Alternatively, when foreign language speakers or writers write or produce metaphors, probably they have already had concepts or ideas rather than linguistic items there in their minds. It is the former rather than the latter that come to their minds first. Linguistic items will be selected only after the formulation of the relevant concepts or ideas. This is the normal process of writing in both L1 and L2 (*cf*. Ma Guanghui 2004). After having conceived some ideas, writers will have the problem of how to put them into words no matter in which language (L1 or L2) they are thinking. There may be two possibilities. When they are able to easily and appropriately find words in their mental lexicon to convey these ideas, successful performances will result. But for foreign language learners, sometimes, if not at all times, they fail to find corresponding or appropriate words or phrases to realize their ideas or concepts because many of them, unlike native speakers, are comparatively linguistically weaker in the target language. Consequently, this incompetence in the target language prevents them from fully expressing what they want to say. Therefore, the power of language proficiency as a prediction factor of metaphor production is reduced. This is considered to be one reason why language proficiency is found to play a less important role than cognitive ability in predicting a significant proportion of the variance of the learners' metaphor production performances.

The aforementioned description of the results indicates just a general correlation between the Chinese EFL learners' cognitive ability and language proficiency and their metaphor comprehension and production performances. Although it confirms the hypothesis that metaphor learning requires both the participation of both cognition and language proficiency, it is just a general tendency and it is unclear how these two factors work when the learners are at different levels of cognition and language proficiency. In other words, it is necessary to cast light on the Chinese EFL learners' metaphor comprehension and production performances when they are at a lower and higher cognitive level and when they are at a lower and higher language proficiency level respectively. And this is the question that the research is to explore in the forthcoming section. For the sake of clarity, the analysis is made of cognition first and then language proficiency.

5.3 Question 2

How do Chinese EFL learners' cognitive ability and language proficiency affect their metaphor comprehension and production when they are at different cognition and language proficiency levels?

5.3.1 Data and analyses

5.3.1.1 Results: Descriptive statistics

In order to address the question put forward above, the present research divided the subjects into two distinct, non-overlapping subgroups according to their levels of cognition and English language proficiency. A tripartite division method was adopted before the dichotomous division. Specifically, the subjects were first divided into three groups based on the subjects' z-scores of their cognitive ability and English proficiency tests, with one third of the subjects from the top, another third from the bottom and one third between the top and the bottom according to their cognitive ability and English proficiency scores. Since the present research was here interested only in whether differences in cognitive ability and language proficiency play distinct roles in metaphor comprehension and production, those whose z-scores were higher than 0.5 were designated members of the high group, those with z-scores less than −0.5 were designated members of the low group. In order to maximize the differences between the groups to make the experiment attain its aim, the subjects whose z-scores lied between −0.5 and 0.5 were eliminated from the examination. Accordingly, the high cognition group (HCG) consisted of 27 subjects and the low cognition group (LCG) was composed of 28 subjects while there were 27 subjects in the high language proficiency group (HPG) and 23 in the low language proficiency group (LPG). The following tables (Table 5.7 and Table 5.8) offer detailed descriptive statistical analyses of the subjects' performances of both cognition and language proficiency groups on the tests in cognition, language proficiency, metaphor comprehension and production. Table 5.7 describes the results of the relevant performances given by the subjects divided by cognition and Table 5.8 is the description of the ones given by the subjects divided by language proficiency.

As is demonstrated in the table below, the mean scores of cognition, language proficiency, metaphor comprehension and production for the LCG are 61.46 (SD = 4.21), 58.28 (SD = 8.04), 40.00 (SD = 11.85) and 2.695 (SD=3.236) respectively. For the HCG, the mean scores of the four variables are 95.259 (SD = 5.834), 71.148 (SD = 4.865), 63.518 (SD = 9.982) and 23.889 (SD = 13.818).

Table 5.7 Descriptive Statistics of Cognition Scores, English Proficiency Scores, Metaphor Comprehension and Production Scores of both HCG and LCG

Variable	LCG(N = 28)				HCG(N = 27)			
	Min	Max	Mean	SD	Min	Max	Mean	SD
COG	50.00	69.00	61.46	4.21	85.00	103.00	95.259	5.834
LP	36.00	69.00	58.28	8.04	61.00	79.00	71.148	4.865
MC	10.00	60.00	40.00	11.85	45.00	80.00	63.518	9.982
MP	.000	10.88	2.695	3.236	4.50	66.75	23.889	13.818

Note: LCG = Low Cognition Group HCG = High Cognition Group
COG = Cognition LP = Language Proficiency MC = Metaphor Comprehension MP = Metaphor Production

Table 5.8 Descriptive Statistics of Cognition Scores, English Proficiency Scores, Metaphor Comprehension and Production Scores of Both HPG and LPG

Variable	LPG(N = 23)				HPG(N = 27)			
	Min	Max	Mean	SD	Min	Max	Mean	SD
COG	57.00	102.0	77.52	12.59	70.00	103.00	87.888	12.279
LP	62.00	68.00	65.56	2.149	71.00	81.00	74.370	3.040
MC	30.00	75.00	55.00	10.552	45.00	80.00	62.777	10.127
MP	.000	36.75	10.811	10.391	.000	65.75	18.985	16.384

Note: LPG = Low Language Proficiency Group HPG = High Language Proficiency Group COG = Cognition LP = Language Proficiency MC = Metaphor Comprehension MP = Metaphor Production

Table 5.8 demonstrates that when the subjects are divided by their language proficiency, their mean scores of cognition, language proficiency, metaphor comprehension and production for the LPG are respectively 77.52 (SD = 12.59), 65.56 (SD= 2.149), 55.00 (SD = 10.552) and 10.811 (SD = 10.391). For the HPG, the mean scores of the four variables are 87.888 (SD = 12.279), 74.370 (SD=3.040), 62.777 (SD=10.127) and 18.985 (SD=16.384).

5.3.2 Metaphor comprehension and production performances of the subjects divided by cognition

In this part, the Chinese EFL learners were divided, based on their cognitive ability, into two groups: the low cognition group (LCG) and high cognition group (HCG). Analyses were made of their cognitive ability scores and their MC and MP performance scores in order to investigate what kind of a relationship lied among the three variables when the subjects were at different level of cognition. For the sake of clarity, the analyses follow the same pattern. In terms of metaphor comprehension and production, the former was considered first then the latter is treated. As regards to cognition group, the analysis was firstly made of the LCG and then followed by the HCG.

5.3.2.1 Metaphor comprehension performances and low cognition

A Pearson correlation analysis was performed in order to see the relationship between the Chinese EFL learners' cognitive ability and language proficiency and their metaphor comprehension performances when they were at a comparatively low level of cognition. The following table (Table 5.9) shows that when the subjects are at a low cognitive level, both their cognitive ability and language proficiency are significantly correlated to their metaphor comprehension scores (cognition and metaphor comprehension: $r = .497$, $p = .007$; language proficiency and metaphor comprehension: $r = .610$, $p = .001$).

Table 5.9 Correlations of the Three Variables of LCG

Variable (N = 28)		COG	LP	MC
COG	Pearson Correlation	1.000	.468	.497
	Sig (2-tailed)		.012	.007
LP	Pearson Correlation	.468	1.000	.610
	Sig (2-tailed)	.012		.001
MC	Pearson Correlation	.497	.610	1.000
	Sig (2-tailed)	.007	.001	

Note: 1. COG = cognition LP = Language Proficiency MC = Metaphor Comprehension Ability

2. Correlation is significant at the 0.05 level (2-tailed).

Since a high correlation was found between the LCG subjects' cognition, language proficiency and their metaphor comprehension performances, it was necessary to see whether the first two variables (cognition and language proficiency) could explain a significant proportion of the variance of metaphor comprehension performances. To achieve this goal, the present research performed a multiple regression analysis with language proficiency and cognition as the independent variables and metaphor comprehension ability as the dependent variable. The findings emerging from the analysis shows that cognition and language proficiency come out together as significant predictors of metaphor comprehension performances ($R^2 = .429$, $F = 9.407$, $p = .001$) (see Table 5.10 below). However, when treated separately, only language proficiency is found to account for a significant proportion of the variance of metaphor comprehension performances ($\beta = .483$, $t = 2.826$, $p = .009$) whereas cognition does not ($\beta = .271$, $t = 1.585$, $p = .126$). Specifically, this means that the learners' language proficiency in the test could predict 48.3% of the variation of their metaphor comprehension performances while the learners' cognition could predict only 27.1% when the learners are at a comparatively low level of cognition.

Table 5.10 A Multiple Regression, Metaphor Comprehension Performance as a Function of Cognition and Language Proficiency (LCG)

Variable	Constant	β	t	R^2	F
COG		.271	1.585		.126
	−42.41			.429	9.407
LP		.483	2.826		.009

Note: COG = level of cognition LP = Language Proficiency MC = Metaphor Comprehension Performance

5.3.2.2 Metaphor comprehension performances and high cognition

In order to investigate the correlation between the subjects' cognitive ability, language proficiency and their metaphor comprehension performances when they were at a high level of cognition, a Pearson correlation was conducted. Table 5.11 shows the relationship. It can be seen from the table that the Chinese EFL learners' cognitive ability and language are differently associated with their metaphor comprehension performances. Specifically, cognition is found to be significantly correlated with metaphor comprehension (r =.459, p =.016) whereas language proficiency is insignificantly correlated (r =.171, p =.394).

Table 5.11 Correlations of the Three Variables of HCG (MC)

Variable (N = 27)		COG	LP	MC
COG	Pearson Correlation	1.000	.249	.459
	Sig (2-tailed)		.210	.016
LP	Pearson Correlation	.249	1.000	.171
	Sig (2-tailed)	.210		.394
MC	Pearson Correlation	.459	.171	1.000
	Sig (2-tailed)	.016	.394	

Note: 1. COG = cognition LP = Language Proficiency MC = Metaphor Comprehension Ability

2. Correlation is significant at the 0.05 level (2-tailed).

To determine to what extent the HCG subjects' cognitive ability and language proficiency could be predictors of their metaphor comprehension, a regression analysis was performed with language proficiency and cognition as the independent variables and metaphor comprehension ability as the dependent variable. The results obtained demonstrate that cognition and language proficiency work together to explain a significant proportion of the variance of the subjects' metaphor comprehension performances (R^2 =.214, F = 3.212, p =.050). Going one step further, the research found that cognition and language proficiency have differential predictive power for the subjects' metaphor comprehension performances. As can be seen in Table 5.12 below, cognition explains a significant proportion of the variance of metaphor comprehension performances (β =.444, t = 2.377, p =.026) while language proficiency does not (β = .060, t =.323, p =.750). In other words, when the subjects are at a relatively high level of cognition, their cognitive ability can predict 44.4% of the variance of their metaphor comprehension performances while the learners' language proficiency can only do 6%.

Table 5.12 A Multiple Regression, Metaphor Comprehension Performance as a Function of Cognition and Language Proficiency (HCG)

Variable	Constant	β	t	R^2	F
COG		.444	2.377		.026
	−17.68			.214	3.212
LP		.060	.323		.750

Note: 1. COG = level of cognition LP = Language Proficiency
MC = Metaphor Comprehension Performance
2.Correlation is significant at the 0.05 level (2-tailed).

Now that the relationship between the Chinese EFL learners' metaphor comprehension and their cognitive ability and language proficiency when they are at both low and high cognitive levels were examined, it was necessary to explore the relationship between the Chinese EFL learners' metaphor production and their cognitive ability and language proficiency when they were at both high and low cognitive levels.

5.3.2.3 Metaphor production performances and low cognition

To explore the correlation between the cognitively low Chinese EFL learners' cognitive ability, language proficiency and their metaphor production performances, the present research performed a Pearson correlation analysis. The results obtained reveal that, of the two variables (cognition and language proficiency), cognition is significantly correlated to the learners' metaphor production performances (r =.534, p =.003) while an insignificant correlation is found between their language proficiency and metaphor production performances (r =.162, p =.411) (See Table 5.13 for details).

Table 5.13 Correlations of the Three Variables of LCG (MP)

Variable (N = 28)		COG	LP	MP
COG	Pearson Correlation	1.000	.468	.534
	Sig (2-tailed)		.012	.003
LP	Pearson Correlation	.468	1.000	.162
	Sig (2-tailed)	.012		.411
MP	Pearson Correlation	.534	.162	1.000
	Sig (2-tailed)	.003	.411	

Note: 1. COG = cognition LP = Language Proficiency MP = Metaphor Production Performances

2. Correlation is significant at the 0.05 level (2-tailed).

Since cognition was found to be highly associated with metaphor production performance whereas language proficiency is not, the research carried out an analysis to see to what extent that cognition and language proficiency can explain the variance of the learners' metaphor production performances. Accordingly, a multiple regression analysis was conducted with language proficiency and cognition as the independent variables and metaphor production performance as the dependent variable. As is indicated in the following table (Table 5.14), the analysis explains a significant proportion of the variance of metaphor production performance (R^2 =.296, F = 5.248, p =.013). However, as far as cognition and language proficiency are treated separately, the predictive power is different. For cognition, the following result is obtained (β =.588, t = 3.093, p =.005), which suggests that cognition accounts for a significant proportion of the variance of the subjects' metaphor production performances. On the contrary, language proficiency is not found to be a significant predictor (β =.113, t =.597, p =.556). Alternatively, when the subjects are at a relatively low level of cognition, their cognitive ability can predict 58.8% of the variance of their metaphor production performances while the learners' language proficiency can only do 11.3%.

Table 5.14 A Multiple Regression, Metaphor Production Performance as a Function of Cognition and Language Proficiency (LCG) (MP)

Variable	Constant	β	t	R^2	F
COG		.588	3.093		.005
	−22.39			.296	5.248
LP		.113	.597		.556

Note: 1. COG = level of cognition LP = Language Proficiency MP = Metaphor Production Performance

2. Correlation is significant at the 0.05 level (2-tailed).

5.3.2.4 Metaphor production performances and high cognition

When the learners are at a relatively high level of cognition, what is the relationship between the Chinese EFL learners' cognitive ability, language proficiency and their metaphor production performances? As is shown by the Pearson correlation study (Table 5.15), the learners' cognitive ability is significantly correlated to their metaphor production performances (r=.487, p=.010) while language proficiency is not (r=.353, p=.071).

Table 5.15 Correlations of the Three Variables of HCG (MP)

Variable (N = 27)		COG	LP	MP
COG	Pearson Correlation	1.000	.249	.487
	Sig (2-tailed)		.210	.010
LP	Pearson Correlation	.249	1.000	.353
	Sig (2-tailed)	.210		.071
MP	Pearson Correlation	.487	.357	1.000
	Sig (2-tailed)	.010	.071	

Note: 1. COG = cognition LP = Language Proficiency MP = Metaphor Production Performances
2. Correlation is significant at the 0.05 level (2-tailed).

In order to investigate whether cognition and language proficiency are significant predictors of the Chinese EFL learners' metaphor production performances, the present research performed a multiple regression analysis using language proficiency and cognition as the independent variables and metaphor production performance as the dependent variable. The results that emerge from the analysis demonstrate that the analysis explains a significant proportion of the variance of metaphor production performance (R^2=.294, F = 4.995, p =.015). The research also made an analysis of the predictive power brought about by cognition and language proficiency on metaphor production performance when the learners were at a comparatively high level of cognition. The results indicate that cognition is found to be a significant factor (β=.425, t=2.401, p=.024) while language proficiency is not (β=.247, t=1.393, p=.176). Put in another way, for cognitively capable learners, their cognitive ability can predict 42.5% of the variance of their metaphor production performances while language proficiency can predict only 24.7%.

Table 5.16 A Multiple Regression, Metaphor Production Performance as a Function of Cognition and Language Proficiency (HCG) (MP)

Variable	Constant	β	t	R^2	F
COG		.425	2.401		.024
	−121.87			.294	4.995
LP		.247	1.393		.176

Note: 1. COG = level of cognition LP = Language Proficiency MP = Metaphor Production Performance

2. Correlation is significant at the 0.05 level (2-tailed).

5.3.2.5 A brief summary

The preceding part is concerned about the analyses of the relationships that exist between cognition, language proficiency and metaphor comprehension and production performances when the learners are divided into two cognitively separate groups: the low group and the high group. Both a correlation analysis and a multiple regression one were conducted of the above-mentioned variables. Several findings emerge from the corresponding analyses.

1) For the cognitively poor learners, metaphor comprehension performance is significantly correlated to both cognition and language proficiency.

2) For the cognitively poor learners, language proficiency is found to be a significant prediction factor of metaphor comprehension while cognition is not.

3) For the cognitively strong learners, metaphor comprehension performance is significantly correlated to cognition whereas it is not highly related to language proficiency.

4) For the cognitively strong learners, cognition is proved to be a significant prediction factor of metaphor comprehension performance while language proficiency is not.

5) For the cognitively poor learners, metaphor production performance is found to be significantly correlated to cognition but insignificantly correlated to language proficiency.

6) For the cognitively poor learners, cognition is found to be a significant predictor of metaphor production performance whereas language proficiency is not.

7) For the cognitively strong learners, metaphor production performance is found to be significantly correlated to cognition while language proficiency is not found to be so.

8) For the cognitively strong learners, cognition is found to be a significant prediction factor of metaphor production performance while language proficiency is not.

A further examination of these eight findings can be summarized into the following general points from the perspectives of correlation and regression analyses. In terms of correlation, cognition is found to be significantly correlated to metaphor comprehension and production performances no matter at what level of cognition the subjects are, while language proficiency is found to be only significantly correlated to metaphor comprehension performances of the cognitively poor learners. In other words, language proficiency is found not to be significantly correlated to metaphor comprehension and production performances of both the cognitively poor and strong learners except to the metaphor comprehension performances of the learners of poor cognition. In view of regression, cognition is found to account for a significant proportion of the variance of metaphor comprehension and production performances of both cognitively poor and strong learners except the metaphor comprehension performances of the cognitively poor learners while language proficiency fail to explain a significant proportion of the variance of the metaphor comprehension and production performances of the learners of both groups except the metaphor comprehension performances of the cognitively poor learners. Rephrasingly, language proficiency is found to be only a significant predictor of the cognitively poor learners' metaphor comprehension performances while cognition is found not to explain a significant proportion of the variance of the metaphor comprehension performances of this group of learners.

5.3.3 Metaphor comprehension and production performances of the subjects divided by language proficiency

In this part, the research performed an analysis of the relationships among the Chinese EFL learners' cognitive ability, language proficiency and their metaphor comprehension and production performances, in which the learners were divided into two groups: the low language proficiency group (LPG) and high language proficiency group (HPG). The aim of the analysis was to see whether the Chinese EFL learners have to attain a certain level of mastery over a requisite linguistic skill before they are able to comprehend and produce metaphors in English. The same procedure was taken as was adopted for the relevant analysis in section 5.3.2.

5.3.3.1 Metaphor comprehension performance and low language proficiency

A Pearson correlation test was run in order to see the relationship between the Chinese EFL learners' cognitive ability and language proficiency and their metaphor comprehension performances when they were at a comparatively low level of language proficiency. It was found that a significant correlation existed between the above-mentioned variables (For cognition: $r = .504$, $p = .014$; for language proficiency: $r = .421$, $p = .046$). The following table (Table 5.17) indicates that when the subjects are at a low language proficiency level, both their cognitive ability and language proficiency are significantly correlated to their metaphor comprehension scores.

Table 5.17 Correlations of the Three Variables of LPG (MC)

Variable (N = 23)		COG	LP	MC
COG	Pearson Correlation	1.000	.400	.504
	Sig (2-tailed)		.059	.014
LP	Pearson Correlation	.400	1.000	.421
	Sig (2-tailed)		.059	.046
MC	Pearson Correlation	.504	.421	1.000
	Sig (2-tailed)	.014	.046	

Note: 1. COG = cognition LP = Language Proficiency MC = Metaphor Comprehension Performance

2. Correlation is significant at the 0.05 level (2-tailed).

As is demonstrated in the above table, a significant correlation was found among the Chinese EFL learners' cognitive ability, language proficiency and their metaphor comprehension performances when they were at a comparatively low level of language proficiency. However, to what extent the first two variables could explain the variance of metaphor comprehension performance was still unknown. To investigate this extent, the present research conducted a multiple regression analysis using language proficiency and cognition as the independent variables and metaphor comprehension performance as the dependent variable. The analysis, as is indicated in Table 5.18 below, accounted for a significant proportion of the variance of English metaphor comprehension performance (R^2 =.565, F = 12.981, p =.000). It can be seen that both cognition and language proficiency emerge as significant factors for predicting metaphor comprehension performances (For cognition: β =.540, t = 3.329, p =.003; for language proficiency: β =.344, t = 2.116, p =.047). It means that when the learners are linguistically poor, cognition can predict 54% of the variance of their metaphor comprehension performance and language proficiency can do 34.4% of the variance.

Table 5.18 A Multiple Regression, Metaphor Comprehension Performance as a Function of Cognition and Language Proficiency (LPG) (MC)

Variable	Constant	β	t	R^2	F
COG		.540	3.329		.003
	−36.171			.565	12.981
LP		.344	2.116	.047	

Note: 1. COG = level of cognition LP = Language Proficiency MC = Metaphor Comprehension Performance

2. Correlation is significant at the 0.05 level (2-tailed).

5.3.3.2 Metaphor comprehension performance and high language proficiency

Both cognition and language proficiency were found to be

significantly correlated to the Chinese EFL learners' metaphor comprehension performances when they were relatively linguistically poor. What is the situation of the kind of relationship when the learners are at a comparatively high level of language proficiency? In order to address the question, a Pearson correlation analysis was performed. It was found that although both cognition and language proficiency are positively correlated to the learners' English metaphor comprehension performance, the correlation is differential for cognition and language proficiency. In other words, cognition is found to be significantly correlated while language proficiency is not (For cognition: r = .404, p =.037; for language proficiency: r =.284, p =.152).

Table 5.19 Correlations of the Three Variables of HPG (MC)

Variable (N = 27)		COG	LP	MC
COG	Pearson Correlation	1.000	.035	.404
	Sig (2-tailed)		.864	.037
LP	Pearson Correlation	.035	1.000	.284
	Sig (2-tailed)	.864		.152
MC	Pearson Correlation	.404	.284	1.000
	Sig (2-tailed)	.037	.152	

Note: 1. COG = cognition LP = Language Proficiency MC = Metaphor Comprehension Performance

2. Correlation is significant at the 0.05 level (2-tailed).

Since cognition was proved to be significantly associated to the learners' English metaphor comprehension performances while language proficiency, though correlated, was not significantly so, then what proportion of the variance of the metaphor comprehension performance could they each explain? To examine it, a multiple regression analysis was run with language proficiency and cognition as the independent variables and metaphor comprehension performance as the dependent variable.

The analysis was found to explain a significant proportion of the variance of English metaphor comprehension performance (R^2 =. 223, F = 3. 446, p =. 048). The results obtained demonstrate that cognition turns out to be a significant predictor of English metaphor comprehension performance (β =.378, t = 2.098, p =.047) while language proficiency can not explain a significant proportion of the variance (β =.289, t = 1.605, p = .121). In other words, cognition can predict 37.8% of the variance of their metaphor comprehension performance and language proficiency can predict only 28.9% of the variance when the learners are relatively linguistically strong.

Table 5.20 A Multiple Regression, Metaphor Comprehension Performance as a Function of Cognition and Language Proficiency (HPG) (MC)

Variable	Constant	β	t	R^2	F
COG		.378	2.098	.047	
	−36.153			.223	3.446
LP		.289	1.605	.121	

Note: 1. COG = level of cognition LP = Language Proficiency MC = Metaphor Comprehension Performance

2. Correlation is significant at the 0.05 level (2-tailed).

The preceding part gives a clear picture of the relationships among the Chinese EFL learners' cognitive ability, English language proficiency and their English metaphor comprehension performances when they are at a comparatively low level of language proficiency. The following parts are going to reveal the relationships among cognition, language proficiency and the learners' English metaphor production performances when they are at a low and high level of language proficiency separately.

5.3.3.3 Metaphor production performance and low language proficiency

The present research conducted a Pearson correlation analysis to investigate the relationships between cognition, language proficiency and the Chinese EFL learners' metaphor production performances when they were relatively linguistically poor. The results obtained from the analysis indicate that both cognition and language proficiency are positively correlated to metaphor production performance. However, cognition is found to be significantly correlated (r =.656, p =.001) while language proficiency is not (r =.077, p =.725).

Table 5.21 Correlations of the Three Variables of LPG (MP)

Variable (N = 23)		COG	LP	MP
COG	Pearson Correlation	1.000	.400	.656
	Sig (2-tailed)		.059	.001
LP	Pearson Correlation	.400	1.000	.077
	Sig (2-tailed)	.059		.725
MP	Pearson Correlation	.656	.077	1.000
	Sig (2-tailed)	.001	.725	

Note: 1. COG = cognition LP = Language Proficiency MP = Metaphor Production Performance
2. Correlation is significant at the 0.05 level (2-tailed).

Since cognition and language proficiency are differentially correlated to metaphor production performance on the level of significance when the learners are relatively poor at language proficiency, then to what extent can they each predict the variance of the metaphor production performance? To answer this question, the research performed a multiple regression analysis.

This regression analysis accounted for a significant proportion of the variance of English metaphor production performance (R^2 =.472, F = 8.922, p =.002). As is seen from the following table (Table 5.22), cognition is found to outperform language proficiency as a significant predictor of the variance of metaphor production performance (For cognition: β =.744, t = 4.197, p =.000; for language proficiency: β =.220, t = 1.242, p = .229). Specifically, cognition is found to predict 74.4% of the variance of their metaphor comprehension performance and language proficiency can predict only 22% of the variance when the learners are relatively linguistically poor.

Table 5.22 A Multiple Regression, Metaphor Production Performance as a Function of Cognition and Language Proficiency (LPG) (MP)

Variable	Constant	β	t	R^2	F
COG		.744	4.197		.000
	−33.012			.472	8.922
LP		.220	1.242		.229

Note: 1. COG = level of cognition LP = Language Proficiency MP = Metaphor Production Performance

2. Correlation is significant at the 0.05 level (2-tailed).

5.3.3.4 Metaphor production performance and high language proficiency

This section is concerned about the relationships existing among the Chinese EFL learners' cognitive ability, language proficiency and their English metaphor production performance when the learners are at a comparatively linguistically strong. A Pearson correlation analysis was first run to investigate the correlation between the three variables. The results obtained suggested that when the learners were at a relatively high level of language proficiency, cognition and language proficiency were found to have a positive correlation to metaphor production performance. Similar to those obtained from the analysis of the correlation between the three variables when the learners were linguistically poor, this analysis demonstrates a positive correlation. It was found that cognition is still significantly correlated to the learners' English metaphor production performances (r =.763, p =.000) while language proficiency, though related, is insignificantly correlated (r =.091, p =.651).

Table 5.23 Correlations of the Three Variables of HPG (MP)

Variable (N = 27)		COG	LP	MP
COG	Pearson Correlation	1.000	−.013	.763
	Sig (2-tailed)		.948	.000
LP	Pearson Correlation	−.013	1.000	.091
	Sig (2-tailed)	.948		.651
MP	Pearson Correlation	.763	.091	1.000
	Sig (2-tailed)	.000	.651	

Note: 1. COG = cognition LP = Language Proficiency MP = Metaphor Production Performance

2. Correlation is significant at the 0.05 level (2-tailed).

In order to investigate what proportion cognition and language proficiency can explain the variance of metaphor production performance when the learners were at a relatively linguistically strong level, a multiple regression analysis was run using language proficiency and cognition as the independent variables and metaphor production performance as the dependent variable.

This regression analysis was found to account for a significant proportion of the variance of English metaphor production performance ($R^2=.592$, $F = 17.414$, $p =.000$). It can be seen from Table 5.24 that cognition can explain a significant proportion of the variance ($\beta =.764$, $t = 5.680$, $p =.000$) while language proficiency turns out to be an insignificant predictor of metaphor production performance ($\beta =.101$, $t =.778$, $p =.444$). This means that cognition can predict 76.48% of the variance of their metaphor comprehension performance and language proficiency can predict only 10.1% of the variance when the learners are relatively linguistically strong.

Table 5.24 A Multiple Regression, Metaphor Production Performance as a Function of Cognition and Language Proficiency (HPG) (MP)

Variable	Constant	β	t	R²	F
COG		.764	5.860		.000
	−112.16			.592	17.414
LP		.101	.778		.444

Note: 1. COG = level of cognition LP = Language Proficiency MP = Metaphor Production Performance

2. Correlation is significant at the 0.05 level (2-tailed).

5.3.3.5 A brief summary

Described in the above part is the examination of the relationships that exist among cognition, language proficiency and English metaphor comprehension and production performances as are measured when the learners are divided into low and high language proficiency groups. The research performed two kinds of analyses (correlation and regression) in order to investigate the relationships between the variables mentioned immediately above, with several findings from the corresponding analyses.

1) For the learners at a comparatively low level of language proficiency, metaphor comprehension performance is positively and significantly correlated to both cognition and language proficiency.

2) For the learners at a comparatively low level of language proficiency, both cognition and language proficiency are found to be significant prediction factors of metaphor comprehension performance.

3) For the learners at a relatively high level of language proficiency, metaphor comprehension performance is positively and significantly correlated to cognition whereas it is insignificantly, though positively, related to language proficiency.

4) For the learners at a relatively high level of language proficiency, cognition is proved to be a significant prediction factor of metaphor comprehension performance while language proficiency is an insignificant prediction factor.

5) For the linguistically poor learners, metaphor production performance is found to be positively and significantly correlated to cognition, but insignificantly, though positively, correlated to language proficiency.

6) For the linguistically poor learners, cognition is found to be a significant predictor of metaphor production performance whereas language proficiency is not.

7) For the linguistically strong learners, metaphor production performance is found to be positively and significantly correlated to cognition while language proficiency is insignificantly related, though positively.

8) For the linguistically strong learners, cognition is found to be a significant prediction factor of metaphor production performance while language proficiency is not.

From the perspectives of correlation and multiple regression analyses, the present research has summarized the above mentioned eight findings into the following relatively general points. In terms of correlation, cognition is found to be consistently positively and significantly correlated to metaphor comprehension and production performances no matter at what level of language proficiency the subjects are, while language proficiency is found to be only positively and significantly correlated to metaphor comprehension performances of the linguistically poor learners. In other words, language proficiency is found not to be significantly correlated to metaphor comprehension and production performances of both the linguistically poor and strong learners except to the metaphor comprehension performances of the learners at a relatively low level of language proficiency. In view of regression, the research has found that cognition accounts for a significant proportion of the variance of metaphor comprehension and production performances of both linguistically poor and strong learners while language proficiency only explains a significant proportion of the variance of the metaphor comprehension performances of the learners at a comparatively low level of language proficiency. Put it in another way, language proficiency can predict a significant proportion of the variance of the linguistically poor learners' metaphor comprehension performances while cognition can consistently predict a significant proportion of the variance of the metaphor comprehension and production performances when the learners are separated into linguistically low and high groups.

5.3.4 A general summary and discussion

5.3.4.1 Summary

Sections 5.3.2 and 5.3.3 are mainly concerned about the relationships that exist among the Chinese EFL learners' cognitive ability, English language proficiency and their English metaphor comprehension and production performances when they are at a comparatively low and high levels of both cognition and language proficiency respectively. After a series of statistical analyses, the present research now makes a general summary of the major findings obtained from the preceding correlation and multiple regression analyses. Summarized in the following are some major findings. As is done earlier, comprehension is treated first and followed by production.

The correlation analyses demonstrate that:

1) For the learners of both low and high cognition and language proficiency groups, cognition is consistently found to be positively and significantly correlated to their metaphor comprehension performances while language proficiency is found to be only positively and significantly correlated to those of the learners who are both cognitively and linguistically poor. In other words, language proficiency is not significantly, though positively, correlated to the metaphor performances of those who are cognitively and linguistically strong.

2) For the learners of both low and high cognition and language proficiency groups, cognition is consistently positively and significantly correlated to their metaphor production performances while language proficiency, though positively, is not significantly so.

The regression analyses show that:

1) For the learners of both low and high cognition and

language proficiency groups except those who are cognitively poor, cognition is proved to be a significant predictor of their metaphor comprehension performances. Language proficiency is found to be a significant predictor of the learners who are both cognitively and linguistically poor. However, it does not predict a significant proportion of the variance of the metaphor comprehension performances of those who are both cognitively and linguistically strong.

2) For the learners of both low and high cognition and language proficiency groups, cognition is consistently found to predict a significant proportion of the variance of the metaphor production performances while language proficiency is not.

5.3.4.2 Discussion

Since the previous analyses are concerned about whether and how the Chinese EFL learners' cognitive ability and language proficiency are correlated to their metaphor comprehension and production performances when the learners are at different cognition and language proficiency levels, the discussions are centered first on the results obtained from the analyses of the relationships between cognition, language proficiency and the performances of the subjects who are cognitively divided, and then on those of the subjects who are divided according to their language proficiency level.

As can be seen from the above analyses, cognition and language proficiency are significantly correlated with the metaphor comprehension performances of the subjects who are cognitively poor. This means that the more competent these learners are in cognition and language proficiency, the more efficiently they perform in comprehending metaphorical sentences. Furthermore, the results indicate that as far as the predictive power is concerned, language proficiency plays a significant role while cognition does not. This is a very interesting finding which might suggest that in comprehending metaphorical sentences, the cognitively poor learners seem to seek more help from their linguistic rather than their cognitive resources. This means that when coming across English metaphors in reading, these cognitively poor readers might often, if not at all times, approach the sentence meanings depending on their knowledge of the basic or literal meanings of the constituent linguistic items. Even when comprehension failure occurs, they either just stop there or are not used to getting over their difficulties with recourse to their cognitive resources even though very likely they may be L1 based. Or even some are willing but cognitively unable to work out the similarity(s) between the things compared. In comparison, when the learners are cognitively competent, their cognitive ability and language proficiency are differently associated with their metaphor comprehension performances. Specifically, cognition plays a highly significant role whereas language proficiency is not. It means that when the learners are at a higher level of cognition, they often very likely work out the meanings of the metaphorical sentences depending on their cognitive effort. On the contrary, the effect of their language proficiency reduces to a significantly low degree. This comparative study apparently shows that cognition and language play different roles in the Chinese EFL learners' metaphor comprehension when they are at different level of cognition. Consequently the data presented in this research has confirmed the finding by Martinez (2003: 33) that language proficiency plays some role in determining whether the figurative meanings of metaphor sentences were accessed. It implies that for foreign language learners, especially those who are cognitively incompetent have to attain a certain level of mastery over a requisite linguistic skill before they are able to comprehend metaphors in English although, as Lakoff & Johnson (1980) hold, metaphor is fundamentally cognitive, and that when these learners become cognitively strong, the effect of language proficiency decreases.

Metaphor production appears to be a different matter. In other words, for both the cognitively poorer and stronger Chinese EFL learners, cognition is consistently found to be significantly associated with their metaphor production performances whereas language proficiency is not. This means that metaphor production, in contrast to metaphor comprehension, is fundamentally more cognitive for the reasons that are present in section 5.2.2.2.

Mention, however, should be made here that although metaphor production was found to be more cognition-driven in the analyses, it does not necessarily mean that the role played by language proficiency can be totally obliterated. This is because that, as the data show, a large percentage of the metaphors the subjects used in this test are mainly attributable to their mastery of the ones they acquired by rote learning from the textbooks. In other words, the subjects used in their compositions some metaphors, but most of which are conventionalized rather than the novel ones, i.e., ones which are produced creatively by the subjects. Alternatively, the subjects may very likely learn these metaphors, consciously or unconsciously, as linguistic combinations rather than spot them as metaphorical language. The data collected provide evidence in support of this assumption because an extremely low frequency of use and low degree of novelty of metaphor are discovered in their compositions. It is, therefore, reasonable not to ignore the role of language proficiency in the process of metaphor production by the Chinese EFL learners.

The analyses demonstrate that when the subjects are divided according to their English language proficiency into two different linguistic levels, i.e., lower and higher groups, broadly similar results emerge as those obtained from the analyses made of the comprehension and production performances of the subjects as are divided by their cognitive ability. This is because generally cognition is highly significantly positively correlated with language proficiency (r =.603, p =.000). Rephrasingly, the subjects who are cognitively competent are also those who are linguistically competent, and vice versa. The results thus suggest that for foreign language learners, especially those who are linguistically incompetent have to attain a certain level of mastery over a requisite linguistic skill before they are able to produce metaphors in English. The reasons are the same as those discussed in the preceding paragraphs. Consequently, no further detailed discussion is needed here again.

In addition to the broadly similar results, the research found something slightly different from those of the above mentioned ones. Specifically, cognition, though correlated with metaphor comprehension performance, was not found to predict a significant proportion of the variance of the metaphor comprehension performances of the poor subjects as were measured by cognition (β =.271, p =.126) whereas it turned out to be a significant predictor of the comprehension performances of the poor subjects as were measured by language proficiency (β=.540, p=.003). This is a finding out of the present researcher's expectation and deserves further investigation.

5.4 Question 3

How do Chinese EFL learners' cognitive ability and language proficiency affect their comprehension of each of the four types of metaphorical sentences and thus affect their performances with respect to the aptness, novelty and density of the metaphor produced?

The question addressed here is aimed to see how the learners' cognitive ability and English language proficiency are related to their comprehension performance of each of the four different types of metaphorical sentences (CFTMS) [(S1: same conceptual metaphor and equivalent linguistic expression; S2: same conceptual metaphor but different linguistic expression; S3: different conceptual metaphors used; S4: words and expressions with similar literal meanings but different metaphorical meanings)], i.e., the four types of sentences that form the entire metaphor comprehension test, and to the density (DEN), aptness (APT) and novelty (NOV) [(PDAN)] of the metaphor generated, i.e., the three component parts that constitute the whole metaphor production test. The following analyses will also begin with metaphor comprehension first and then metaphor production.

5.4.1 Data and data analyses

5.4.1.1 Results: descriptive statistics

Table 5.25 Descriptive Statistics of the Scores for COG, LP, CFTMS and PDAN

Variable (N = 82)				
	Min	Max	Mean	SD
COG	50.00	103.00	77.13	14.76
LP	36.00	81.00	66.07	8.42
S1	10.00	25.00	22.19	3.24
S2	.00	25.00	17.31	5.45
S3	.00	15.00	5.36	4.42
S4	.00	20.00	8.11	5.31
Den	.00	4.75	.99	1.02
APT	.00	47.00	8.30	9.05
NOV	.00	14.00	2.04	3.10

Note: COG = Cognition LP = Language Proficiency S1 = the First

Type of Metaphorical Sentence S2 = the Second Type of Metaphorical Sentence S3 = the Third Type of Metaphorical Sentence S4 = the Fourth Type of Metaphorical Sentence DEN = Metaphor Density APT = Metaphor Aptness NOV = Metaphor Novelty

Described in the above are the statistics of cognition scores, English language proficiency scores, the scores for the comprehension performance of each of the four different types of metaphorical sentences and the scores for their performance of the three component parts (density, aptness and novelty). The four types of metaphorical sentences are abbreviated as S1, S2, S3 and S4 while the three component parts of metaphor production test are shortened as DEN, APT and NOV respectively.

5.4.1.2 Results for COG, LP and CFTMS: a correlation analysis

A Pearson correlation analysis was performed in order to study the relationships that exist among the Chinese EFL learners' cognitive ability, language proficiency and the comprehension performances of the four types of metaphorical sentences. The results obtained from the analysis indicated that there was a significant correlation between the aforementioned variables. Specifically, both cognition and language proficiency were found to be significantly positively correlated to the subjects' comprehension performance of each of the four types of metaphorical sentence. The correlation coefficients are stated respectively as follows [COG and S1: (r =.465, p =.000), LP and S1: (r =.552, p =.000); COG and S2: (r =.480, p =.000), LP and S2: (r =.555, p =.000); COG and S3: (r =.601, p =.000), LP and S3: (r =.543, p =.000); COG and S4: (r =.600, p =.000), LP and S4: (r =.549, p =.000).

Table 5.26 Correlations of COG, LP and Comprehension Performances of S1, S2, S3 and S4

Variable (N = 82)		S1	S2	S3	S4
COG	Pearson Correlation	.465	.480	.601	.600
	Sig (2-tailed)	.000	.000	.000	.000
LP	Pearson Correlation	.552	.555	.543	.549
	Sig (2-tailed)	.000	.000	.000	.000

Note: 1. COG = cognition LP = Language Proficiency S1 = the First Type of Metaphorical Sentence S2 = the Second Type of Metaphorical Sentence S3 = the Third Type of Metaphorical Sentence S4 = the Fourth Type of Metaphorical Sentence

2. Correlation is significant at the 0.01 level (2-tailed).

5.4.1.3 Results for the relationships between COG, LP and S1 comprehension performance: a regression analysis

Since a significantly positive correlation was found, the research would conduct a series of regression analyses in order to investigate whether the subjects' cognitive ability, language proficiency could explain a significant proportion of the variances of the comprehension performance of each of the four types of metaphorical sentences respectively using the first two variables (cognition and language proficiency) as independent ones and the comprehension performance of each of the four types of metaphorical sentences as dependent ones.

Table 5. 27 provides a definite description of the results obtained from the regression analysis of the subjects' cognitive ability, language proficiency and their comprehension performance of the first type of metaphorical sentences. It can be found in the table that this analysis can account for a significant proportion of the variance of the comprehension performance of the first type of metaphorical sentences (R^2 =.332, F = 19.623, p =.000). However, of the two independent variables, language proficiency outperforms cognition as the only significant predictor (for language proficiency: β =.427, t = 3.703, p =.000; for cognition: β =.207, t = 1.797, p =.078). This means that language proficiency can explain 42.7% of the variance of the subjects' comprehension performances of the first type of metaphorical sentences while cognition can only predict 20.7%.

Table 5.27 A Multiple Regression, Comprehension Performance of S1 as a Function of Cognition and Language Proficiency

Variable	Constant	β	t	R^2	F
COG		.207	1.797		.076
	7.875			.332	19.623
LP		.427	3.703		.000

Note: 1. COG = level of cognition LP = Language Proficiency

2. Correlation is significant at the 0.05 level (2-tailed).

5.4.1.4 Results for the relationships between COG, LP and S2 comprehension performance: a regression analysis

Described in the following table (Table 5.28) is the description of the results obtained from the regression analysis of the subjects' cognitive ability, language proficiency and their comprehension performance of the second type of metaphorical sentences. The result shows that this analysis explains a significant proportion of the variance of the comprehension performance of the second type of metaphorical sentences (R^2=.342, F=20.500, p=.000). It can be found that, different from the result of what is done in the above, both cognition and language proficiency turn out to be significant predictors of the variance of the subjects' comprehension performances of the second type of metaphorical sentences (For cognition: β =.229, t = 1.998, p =.049; for language proficiency: β =.417, t = 3.648, p =.000). It is meant that 22.9% of the variance of the subjects' comprehension performance of the second type of metaphorical sentences is associated with cognition while 41.27% is contributed by language proficiency.

Table 5.28 A Multiple Regression, Comprehension Performance of S2 as a Function of Cognition and Language Proficiency

Variable	Constant	β	t	R^2	F
COG		.229	1.998		.049
	−6.933			.342	20.500
LP		.4127	3.648		.000

Note: 1. COG = level of cognition LP = Language Proficiency

2. Correlation is significant at the 0.05 level (2-tailed).

5.4.1.5 Results for the relationship between COG, LP and S3 comprehension performance: a regression analysis

A multiple regression analysis was run to investigate the roles played by cognition and language proficiency in the subjects' comprehension performance of the third type of metaphorical sentence. Table 5.29 shows that this regression analysis explains a significant proportion of the variance of the comprehension performances of the sentences (R^2 =.413, F = 27.765, p = .000). Specifically, both independent variables can significantly predict the variance of the dependent variable (for cognition: β =.430, t = 3.980, p =.000; for language proficiency: β =. 284, t = 2.625, p =.010). This result indicates that 43% of the variance of the comprehension performance of the third type of metaphorical sentences is explained by cognition while 28.4% is done by language proficiency.

Table 5.29 A Multiple Regression, Comprehension Performance of S3 as a Function of Cognition and Language Proficiency

Variable	Constant	β	t	R^2	F
COG		.430	3.980		.000
	−14.374			.413	27.765
LP		.284	2.625		.010

Note: 1. COG = level of cognition LP = Language Proficiency
2. Correlation is significant at the 0.05 level (2-tailed).

5.4.1.6 Results for the relationship between COG, LP and S4 comprehension performance: a regression analysis

In order to investigate the relationship of the subjects' cognitive ability and language proficiency to their comprehension performance of the fourth type of metaphorical sentences, a multiple regression analysis was performed. The result is shown in Table 5.30 below. According to the table, this analysis accounts for a significant proportion of the variance of the comprehension performance of the sentences (R^2=.415, F = 28.030, p =.000). It can be seen that two independent variables together can significantly predict the variance of the dependent variable (for cognition: β =. 423, t = 3. 922, p =. 000; for language proficiency: β =.294, t = 2.722, p =.008). It means that cognition can predict 42.3% of the variance of the comprehension performance of the fourth type of metaphorical sentence while language proficiency can do 29.4%.

Table 5.30 A Multiple Regression, Comprehension Performance of S4 as a Function of Cognition and Language Proficiency

Variable	Constant	β	t	R^2	F
COG		.423	3.922		.000
	−15.761			.415	28.030
LP		.294	2.722		.008

Note: 1. COG = level of cognition LP = Language Proficiency

2. Correlation is significant at the 0.05 level (2-tailed)

5.4.1.7 Results for COG, LP and PDAN: a correlation analysis

The research conducted a correlation analysis to examine the relationship between the Chinese EFL learners' cognitive ability, language proficiency and their performance of metaphor density (DEN), aptness (APT) and novelty (NOV). The following table (Table 5.31) shows the correlations among them. It can be found that there are quite significantly positive correlations between the variables concerned. The coefficients are given respectively [COG and DEN: (r =.691, p =.000), LP and DEN: (r =.349, p = .001); COG and APT: (r =.775, p =.000), LP and APT: (r = .396, p =.000); COG and NOV: (r =.714, p =.000), LP and NOV: (r =.347, p =.001)].

Table 5.31 Correlations of COG, LP and Production Performances of DEN, APT and NOV

Variable (N = 82)		DEN	APT	NOV
COG	Pearson Correlation	.691	.775	.714
	Sig (2-tailed)	.000	.000	.000
LP	Pearson Correlation	.349	.396	.347
	Sig (2-tailed)	.001	.000	.001

Note: 1. COG = cognition LP = Language Proficiency DEN = Density
APT = Aptness NOV = Novelty
2. Correlation is significant at the 0.01 level (2-tailed).

Since a highly significant correlation was found among the subjects' cognitive ability, language proficiency and their performance of metaphor density, aptness and novelty, a regression analysis was conducted to examine how the two independent variables (cognition and language proficiency) were associated with the dependant variables (performance of metaphor density, aptness and novelty) respectively.

5.4.1.8 Results for the relationship between COG, LP and DEN: a regression analysis

In order to examine the relationships that exist between the Chinese EFL learners' cognitive ability, language proficiency and their performance of metaphor density, a multiple regression analysis was carried out. The analysis was found to account for a significant proportion of the variance of the production performance of metaphor density (R^2 =.485, F = 37.146, p = .000). However, of the two independent variables, cognition was seen to be a highly significant predictor of the variance of the subjects' production performance of metaphor density (β =.755, t = 7.459, p =.000) while language proficiency was not (β = −.107, t = −1.052, p =.296). This means that cognition can predict 75.5% of the variance of the production performance of metaphor density language proficiency can not.

Table 5.32 A Multiple Regression, Performance of Metaphor Density as a Function of Cognition and Language Proficiency

Variable	Constant	β	t	R^2	F
COG		.755	7.459		.000
	−2.201			.485	37.146
LP		−.107	−1.052		.296

Note: 1. COG = level of cognition LP = Language Proficiency

2. Correlation is significant at the 0.05 level (2-tailed)

5.4.1.9 Results for the relationship between COG, LP and APT: a regression analysis

Another multiple regression analysis was run to investigate whether the subjects' cognitive ability and language proficiency were significant predictors of their performance of English metaphor aptness using cognition and language proficiency as the prediction variables and performance of metaphor aptness as the criterion variable. The results obtained indicate that this analysis explains a significant proportion of the variance of the performance of metaphor aptness (R^2 =.609, F = 61.592, p = .000). The two prediction factors were found to account for different proportions of the variance of the dependent variable. In other words, cognition can predict a significant proportion of the variance of the performance of metaphor aptness (β =.843, t = 9.562, p =.000) while language proficiency can not (β =−.112, t = −1.272, p =.207). Table 5.33 below demonstrates the relationships.

Table 5.33 A Multiple Regression, Performance of Metaphor Aptness as a Function of Cognition and Language Proficiency

Variable	Constant	β	t	R^2	F
COG		.843	9.562		.000
	−23.640			.609	61.592
LP		−.112	−1.272		.207

Note: 1. COG = level of cognition LP = Language Proficiency
2. Correlation is significant at the 0.05 level (2-tailed)

5.4.1.10 Results for the relationship between COG, LP and NOV: a regression analysis

The research conducted a multiple regression analysis in order to examine whether the Chinese EFL learners' cognitive ability and language proficiency could predict a significant proportion of the variance of their performance of English metaphor novelty. The analysis was found to account for a significant proportion of the variance of the dependent variable (R^2 = .515, F = 41.983, p = .000). However, cognition and language proficiency were found to play quite different roles in predicting the proportion of the variance of the performance of metaphor novelty. Specifically, it can be seen from Table 5.34 below that cognition explains a highly significant proportion (β = .768, t = 7.823, p = .000) whereas language proficiency does not (β = −.090, t = −.912, p = .364). This means that cognition can explain 76.8% of the variance of the subjects' performance of metaphor novelty, but language proficiency does not.

Table 5.34 A Multiple Regression, Performance of Metaphor Novelty as a Function of Cognition and Language Proficiency

Variable	Constant	β	t	R^2	F
COG		.768	7.823		.000
	−8.249			.515	41.983
LP		−.090	−.912		.364

Note: 1. COG = level of cognition LP = Language Proficiency

2. Correlation is significant at the 0.05 level (2-tailed)

5.4.2 Summary and discussion

5.4.2.1 Summary

The preceding parts deal with the relationships that exist among cognition, language proficiency and the metaphor comprehension performance of each of the four types of metaphorical sentences and the performance of metaphor density, aptness and novelty from the correlation and regression analyses respectively. The research has come up with several findings, which are summarized in the following.

The corresponding correlation analyses demonstrate that:

1) Both the subjects' cognitive ability and English language proficiency are highly significantly associated with their comprehension performance of each of the four types of metaphorical sentences.

2) Cognition seems to be more related to the comprehension performance of S3 and S4 while language proficiency to S1 and S2.

3) Both the subjects' cognitive ability and English language proficiency are highly significantly correlated with their performance of metaphor density, aptness and novelty.

The relevant multiple regression analyses indicate that:

1) The subjects' English language proficiency is a highly

significant predictor for the comprehension performance of each of the four types of metaphorical sentence and their cognitive ability is a significant predictor of those of the last three sentences (i.e., S2, S3 and S4) except the first one. That is to say, the subjects' cognitive ability can not account for a significant proportion of the variance of the comprehension performance of the first type of metaphorical sentences.

2) Cognition seems to predict a more significant proportion of the variance of the comprehension performance of the third and fourth types of metaphorical sentences while language proficiency appears to have a more powerful effect on the comprehension performance of the first and second.

3) The subjects' cognitive ability can explain a very significant proportion of the variance of their performance of metaphor density, aptness and novelty whereas their English language proficiency can not.

An in-depth examination of the previously stated findings can be summarized into the following general points from the perspectives of correlation and regression analyses. The findings from the correlation analyses are quite the same for both metaphor comprehension and production. In other words, the Chinese EFL learners' cognitive ability and language proficiency are unanimously significantly correlated with their comprehension performance of each of the four types of metaphorical sentences and performance of metaphor density, aptness and novelty. The multiple regression analyses show that the subjects' cognitive ability can predict a significant proportion of the variance of their production performance of metaphor density, aptness and novelty as well as their comprehension performance of the last three types of metaphorical sentences with the exception of the first type. The analyses also indicate that the Chinese EFL learners' language proficiency is a significant prediction factor of the comprehension performance of the four types of metaphorical sentences whereas it is not the one of the performance of metaphor density, aptness and novelty.

5.4.2.2 Discussion

The results obtained from the previous analyses are discussed here. As usual, the discussions are made of the relationships that exist among the subjects' cognitive ability, language proficiency and their performance in comprehending each of the four different types of metaphorical sentences, and then of the ones that lie among the subjects' cognitive ability, language proficiency and their performance of metaphor density, aptness and novelty.

5.4.2.2.1 Discussion about metaphor comprehension

These results are quite similar to those obtained from the correlation analyses made between the first two variables (cognition and language proficiency) and the comprehension performance of the metaphorical sentences taken as a whole. The results, thus, provide the question raised above with a convincing answer: the Chinese EFL learners' cognitive ability and language proficiency are significantly correlated to their comprehension performance of each of the four types of metaphorical sentences. This means that when the subjects read each of the four types of metaphorical sentences, the higher their cognitive ability and language proficiency are, the better their comprehension performance of each of the four types of metaphorical sentences is, and vice versa. Moreover, it was found that cognition is more related to the comprehension performance of the sentences with different conceptual metaphors in Chinese and English and that language proficiency is more correlated to the sentences whose concepts are equivalent and linguistic expressions are different in the two languages.

The multiple regression analyses offer a more complicated picture of the prediction power held by cognition and language proficiency on the comprehension performance of each of the four types of metaphorical sentences. Though complicated, the results further confirm the above mentioned conclusion: cognition and language proficiency are significantly involved in the metaphor comprehension process because the analyses explain a significant proportion of the variance of the performance when the two independent variables are combined together. Moreover, the research has found that when the two independent variables (cognition and language proficiency) were processed separately, the roles played by each were somewhat different in the Chinese EFL learners' reading process of each of the four types of metaphorical sentences. This seems to suggest that when foreign language learners read metaphorical sentences, they have recourse to both their cognitive and linguistic knowledge in order to reach a correct understanding of the sentences read. This also suggests that the learners' cognitive ability contributes more to the understanding of the sentences with different conceptual metaphors. However, it does not mean that their language proficiency remains dormant or inactive there while reading. It is assumed that foreign language learners get recourse first to the literal meanings of the linguistic expressions and only when failure occurs they fall back upon their cognitive resources to infer the meanings of the sentences relying on their knowledge of the literal meanings of the related linguistic expressions. Understanding occurs when their cognitive effort is successful, and vice versa. Mention should be made here that although foreign language learners may first depend on their knowledge of the literal meanings of the linguistic expressions in order to comprehend the sentences with different conceptual metaphors, their cognitive ability seems to play a more crucial role. This is because even if they are familiar with the literal meanings of the linguistic expressions concerned, they, unlike native speakers, might not be so cognitively conscious and capable as to work out the metaphorical meanings of the linguistic expressions, i.e., the similarities between the things compared, especially when the two languages or cultures differ considerably.

A comparison of the difficulty degree of the four types of metaphorical sentence provides another piece of evidence for the assumptions discussed above. As can be seen from the following table (Table 5.35) that the mean scores of each type of the metaphorical sentences are 22.195 for the first type, 17.317 for the second, 5.365 for the third and 8.109 for the fourth, there exist significant differences between the four types of metaphorical sentences ($F=229.773$, $p=.000$). A significance level of < 0.05 the Scheffe test showed that significant differences were between S1 and S2 ($<.000$), S2 and S3 ($<.000$), S1 and S3 ($<.000$) and S1 and S4 ($<.000$), S3 and S4 ($<.003$). In S1, metaphorical units with shared conceptual basis and equivalent linguistic form proved to be easiest. The combined score for S2 was the second highest after S1, which indicated that metaphorical sentences with same conceptual basis but different linguistic form were a little more difficult than S1 for the subjects to understand. S3 proved to be hardest because the subjects scored the lowest, which suggests that when the conceptual bases are different between the two languages, big difficulty arises for foreign language learners. S4 scored the second lowest, which implied that the sentences with similar literal meanings but different metaphorical meanings are comparatively easier to understand than the ones whose conceptual bases are completely different. The research seemed to find evidence in support of the one performed by Charteris-Black (2002). In other words, the metaphorical sentences which are both conceptually and linguistically different are the hardest for the Chinese EFL learners to understand and vice versa. Moreover, the sentences with different concepts and similar linguistic expressions are more difficult than those with similar concepts and different linguistic expressions. Therefore, it can be inferred that in reading the metaphorical sentences, the Chinese EFL learners will most likely process the literal meanings of the linguistic expression first and only when failure occurs, they seek help from their cognitive resources, which in turn proves that both cognition and language proficiency are involved in the comprehension of each type of metaphorical sentences.

Table 5.35 Descriptive Statistics of the Mean Scores for Each of the Four Types of Metaphorical Sentence

Variable (N = 82)				
	Min	Max	Mean	SD
S1	10.00	25.00	22.195	3.24
S2	.00	25.00	17.317	5.45
S3	.00	15.00	5.365	4.42
S4	.00	20.00	8.109	5.31

Note: S1 = the First Type of Metaphorical Sentence S2 = the Second Type of Metaphorical Sentence S3 = the Third Type of Metaphorical Sentence S4 = the Fourth Type of Metaphorical Sentence

5.4.2.2.2 Discussion about metaphor production

The correlation analyses show that both cognition and language proficiency are significantly correlated with the density, aptness and novelty of the metaphors generated by the Chinese

EFL learners. It follows that the more competent the learners are in their cognitive ability and language proficiency, the more successfully they perform with respect to the density, aptness and novelty of the metaphors produced. What is more, cognition seems to be more related than language proficiency to their performances of each of the items concerned.

The multiple regression analyses seem to demonstrate that the Chinese EFL learners' cognitive ability and language proficiency can jointly account for a significant proportion of the variation of their performance of the density, aptness and novelty of the metaphors generated. It suggests that cognition intermingled with language proficiency can bring about success in dealing with the density, aptness and novelty of the metaphors generated by the learners. However, when processed separately, cognition was found to have a significant predictive power on the subjects' performance of the three dependent variables whereas language proficiency did not. This implies that the cognitively stronger EFL learners are, the more metaphors they use or create and the better they will make about the metaphors produced with respect to aptness and novelty. This process is, to a greater extent, cognition or concept determined because the subjects do think in terms of concepts instead of linguistic expressions no matter in which language, either in L1 or L2, they do their thinking. Only when they have successfully made clear of what they are going to express, do they start to select linguistic expressions to convey the ideas (or sometimes concepts and linguistic expressions might go synchronically, but generally and fundamentally it is concepts not linguistic items that bring out and guide the thinking process). And in this case, they most likely choose in their mental lexicon the corresponding linguistic expressions that they can find or with which they are familiar to express themselves. Sometimes, if they fail to sort out one that can be used to describe what they intend to express metaphorically so aptly or freshly, they will have to express the idea concerned literally. Further mention should be made here especially for some advanced learners that even if they intend to express their ideas metaphorically after working out the similarities between the things compared, inhibition of metaphorical expression may occur when they are not so sure of whether their expression is cross-culturally contradictory or acceptable because some of them are well aware that complete transfer of concept and/or linguistic forms sometimes results in communicative awkwardness or failure. In other words, when this happens, learners will probably sacrifice vividness for the sake of exactness. This, the present research believes, can at least partially explain why language proficiency was found to be significantly correlated with metaphor production as are measured by density, aptness and novelty but to insignificantly predict the variation of the metaphor production performance of the Chinese EFL learners.

5.5 Question 4

To what extent do Chinese EFL learners with varying degrees of cognitive and linguistic ability differ in their comprehension of the four types of metaphorical sentence and differ with respect to the density, aptness and novelty of the metaphor generated?

5.5.1 Data and data analyses

5.5.1.1 Results: descriptive statistics

In order to address the questions put forward above, the present research divided the eighty two subjects, based on the levels of their cognitive and linguistic ability respectively, into three cognition and three language proficiency groups with the subjects whose z-scores were higher than 0.5 as the top, those whose z-scores were less than －0.5 as the low and those in-between as the intermediate. Consequently, the three cognition groups consist of 27 (HCG), 27 (ICG) and 28 subjects (LCG) respectively and the three language proficiency are composed of 27 (HLG), 32 (ILG) and 23 (LLG) subjects respectively. The following tables (Table 5.36 and Table 5.37) offer detailed descriptive statistical analyses of the subjects' performances of each variables concerned.

Table 5.36 Descriptive Statistics of the Performances of the Three Cognition Groups

	HCG (N=27)		ICG (N=27)		LCG (N=28)	
	Mean	SD	Mean	SD	Mean	SD
S1	23.88	2.11	22.22	2.88	20.54	3.68
S2	19.82	4.27	18.89	4.45	13.39	5.27
S3	8.15	3.95	6.67	3.67	1.43	2.30
S4	11.67	5.18	8.15	4.41	4.64	3.83
DEN	1.89	1.19	.77	.58	.39	.38
APT	17.04	9.57	5.93	5.56	2.18	2.61
NOV	4.96	3.54	1.07	1.94	.178	.390

LCG = Low Cognition Group ICG = Intermediate Cognition Group HCG = High Cognition Group S1 = Type 1 sentences S2 = Type 2 sentences S3 = Type 3 sentences S4 = Type 4 sentences DEN = Density APT = Aptness NOV = Novelty

Table 5.37 Descriptive Statistics of the Performances of the Three Language Proficiency Groups

	HCG (N=27)		ICG (N=32)		LCG (N=23)	
	Mean	SD	Mean	SD	Mean	SD
S1	23.51	2.32	22.34	2.83	20.43	3.96
S2	19.63	4.36	18.44	4.47	13.04	5.58
S3	8.33	3.39	5.31	4.20	1.96	3.28
S4	11.48	5.33	7.97	3.98	4.35	4.34
DEN	1.89	1.19	.77	.58	.39	.38
APT	17.04	9.57	5.93	5.56	2.18	2.61
NOV	4.96	3.54	1.07	1.94	.178	.390

Note: HLG = High Language Proficiency Group ILG = Intermediate Language Proficiency Group LLG = Low Language Proficiency Group S1 = Type 1 sentences S2 = Type 2 sentences S3 = Type 3 sentences S4 = Type 4 sentences DEN = Density APT = Aptness NOV = Novelty

5.5.1.2 Results: Effects of different levels of cognitive and linguistic ability on comprehending the four types of metaphorical sentences

In order to further investigate what differences the Chinese EFL learners of different cognitive ability with different linguistic ability make in their comprehension of the four different types of metaphorical sentences, the present research conducted a 3 x 4 x 3 mixed-design ANOVA on the metaphor comprehension scores, with two between-subjects factors: cognition group (CG) (low, intermediate, high) and language proficiency group (LG) (low, intermediate, high) and one within-subject factor: sentence type (four types).

The ANOVA analysis (Table 5.38) shows that the subjects'

cognitive ability, linguistic ability and the sentence type all had main effects (cognitive ability: *F* (1, 328) = 15.600, *p* =.000; linguistic ability: *F* (1, 328) = 3.472, *p* =.032; sentence type: *F* (1, 328) = 217.513, *p* =.000). It is demonstrated that a significant two-way interaction exists between the subjects' cognitive ability and linguistic ability (*F* (1, 328) = 2.701, *p* = .046). In addition, it can be seen that no significant interaction effect exists among the three factors (*F* (1, 328) =.827, *p* = .592).

Table 5.38 ANOVA Results with Between-subjects Factors, Cognition and Language Proficiency Group and Within-subjects Factor, Comprehension of Metaphors

Dependent Variable: Scores of metaphor comprehension

Source	TypeIII Sum of Squares	df	Mean Square	F	Sig.
Corrected Model	17890.049	31	577.098	38.587	.000
Intercept	37709.918	1	37709.918	2521.406	.000
LG	103.859	2	51.930	3.472	.032
SENTYPE	9759.294	3	325.098	217.513	.000
CG	466.614	2	233.307	15.600	.000
LG CG	121.173	3	40.391	2.701	.046
LG CG SENTYPE	111.329	9	12.370	.827	.592
Error	4426.948	296	14.956		
Total	79875.000	328			
Corrected Total	22316.997	327			

a R Squared =.802 (Adjusted R Squared =.781)

Note: LG = Language Proficiency Group CG = Cognition Group
SENTYPE =The Four Types of Metaphorical Sentence

5.5.1.3 Results: Effects of different levels of cognitive and linguistic ability on comprehending the first type of metaphorical sentences

The research conducted an ANOVA to examine whether the subjects of different cognitive ability with different language proficiency differ in their comprehension of the first type of metaphorical sentences. It can be seen from the table below (Table 5. 39) that the subjects' cognitive ability, language proficiency did not have main effects (cognitive ability: F (1, 82) = 2.231, p =.115; language proficiency: F (1, 28) =.341, p = .712). The table also shows that an insignificant two-way interaction exists between the subjects' cognitive ability and language proficiency (F (1, 28) =.612, p =.609).

Table 5.39 ANOVA Results with Between-subjects Factors, Cognition and Language Proficiency Group and Within-subjects Factor, Comprehension of the First Type of Metaphorical Sentence

Dependent Variable: Scores of S1 comprehension

Source	TypeIII Sum of Squares	df	Mean Square	F	Sig.
Corrected Model	188.199	7	26.886	2.984	.008
Intercept	26116.129	1	26116.129	2898.837	.000
CG	40.197	2	20.097	2.231	.115
LG	6.141	2	3.070	.341	.712
CG LG	16.539	3	5.513	.612	.609
Error	666.679	74	9.009		
Total	79875.000	82			
Corrected Total	854.878	81			

a R Squared =.220 (Adjusted R Squared =.146)

Note: LG = Language Proficiency Group CG = Cognition Group S1 = The First Type of Metaphorical Sentence

5.5.1.4 Results: Effects of different levels of cognitive and linguistic ability on comprehending the second type of metaphorical sentences

A similar analysis was carried out to examine whether the subjects of different cognitive ability with different language proficiency differ in their comprehension of the second type of metaphorical sentence. The results (Table 5.40) indicate that cognitive ability had main effect (F (1, 82) = 4.459, p =.015) whereas language proficiency did not (F (1, 28) = 1.404, p = .252). Moreover, no significant two-way interaction effect was found between cognitive and language proficiency.

Table 5.40 ANOVA Results with Between-subjects Factors, Cognition and Language Proficiency Group and Within-subjects Factor, Comprehension of the Second Type of Metaphorical Sentences

Dependent Variable: Scores of S2 comprehension

Source	TypeIII Sum of Squares	df	Mean Square	F	Sig.
Corrected Model	858.938	7	122.705	5.855	.008
Intercept	16269.998	1	16269.998	776.351	.000
CG	186.887	2	93.443	4.459	.015
LG	58.840	2	29.420	1.404	.252
CG LG	88.651	3	29.550	1.410	.247
Error	1550.818	74	20.957		
Total	27000.000	82			
Corrected Total	2409.756	81			

a R Squared =.356 (Adjusted R Squared =.296)

Note: LG = Language Proficiency Group CG = Cognition Group S2 = The Second Type of Metaphorical Sentences

5.5.1.5 Results: Effects of different levels of cognitive and linguistic ability on comprehending the third type of metaphorical sentences

The research carried out an ANOVA to investigate whether the subjects of different cognitive ability with different language proficiency differ in their comprehension of the third type of metaphorical sentences. A nearly same result was found (Table 5.41) as that in the preceding analysis. Specifically, cognitive ability consistently had main effect (F (1, 82) = 11.272, p = .000) while language proficiency did not (F (1, 28) = 1.124, p =.331). However, this time the research found a significant two-way interaction effect between cognitive ability and language proficiency, which was different from the above two corresponding analyses (F (1, 82) = 3.431, p =.021).

Table 5.41 ANOVA Results with Between-subjects Factors, Cognition and Language Proficiency Group and Within-subjects Factor, Comprehension of the Third Type of Metaphorical Sentences

Dependent Variable: Scores of S3 comprehension

Source	TypeIII Sum of Squares	df	Mean Square	F	Sig.
Corrected Model	832.953	7	118.993	11.646	.000
Intercept	1652.481	1	1652.481	161.735	.000
CG	230.336	2	115.168	11.272	.000
LG	22.964	2	11.482	1.124	.331
CG LG	105.177	3	35.059	3.431	.021
Error	756.072	74	10.217		
Total	3950.000	82			
Corrected Total	1589.024	81			

a R Squared =.524 (Adjusted R Squared =.479)

Note: LG = Language Proficiency Group CG = Cognition Group S3 =

The Third Type of Metaphorical Sentences

5.5.1.6 Results: Effects of different levels of cognitive and linguistic ability on comprehending the fourth type of metaphorical sentences

An ANOVA was run to see whether the subjects of different cognitive ability with different linguistic ability differ in their comprehension of the fourth type of metaphorical sentences. It can be seen from Table 5.42 that cognitive ability had main effect (F (1, 82) = 174.672, p =.000) whereas language proficiency did not (F (1, 28) = 2.630, p =.079). But the analysis did not find a significant two-way interaction effect between cognitive ability and language proficiency F (1, 82) =.376, p =.771).

Table 5.42 ANOVA Results with Between-subjects Factors, Cognition and Language Proficiency Group and Within-subjects Factor, Comprehension of the Fourth Type of Metaphorical Sentences

Dependent Variable: Scores of S4 comprehension

Source	TypeIII Sum of Squares	df	Mean Square	F	Sig.
Corrected Model	828.632	7	118.376	6.027	.000
Intercept	3430.604	1	3430.604	174.672	.000
CG	103.305	2	51.653	2.630	.079
LG	69.326	2	34.663	1.765	.178
CG LG	22.135	3	7.378	.376	.771
Error	1453.380	74	19.640		
Total	7675.000	82			
Corrected Total	2282.012	81			

a R Squared =.363 (Adjusted R Squared =.303)

Note: LG = Language Proficiency Group CG = Cognition Group S4 = The Fourth Type of Metaphorical Sentences

5.5.1.7 Results: Effects of different levels of cognitive and linguistic ability on metaphor density

In order to examine to what extent the Chinese EFL learners with varying degrees of cognitive and linguistic ability differ with respect to the density of the metaphor generated, the present research performed a 3 x 3 mixed-design ANOVA on the scores the subjects achieved with respect to density, with two between-subjects factors: cognition group (CG) (low, intermediate, high) and language proficiency group (LG) (low, intermediate, high) and one within-subject factor: density of the metaphor generated. The ANOVA results (Table 5.43) show that the subjects' cognitive ability had main effect (F (2, 82) = 12.021, p =.000) whereas language proficiency did not have (F (2, 82) =.265, p =.768). Moreover, no two-way interaction was found between cognitive ability and language proficiency (F (2, 82) = 1.544, p =.210).

Table 5.43 ANOVA Results with Between-subjects Factors, Cognition and Language Proficiency Group and Within-subjects Factor, Metaphor Density

Dependent variable: Density

Source	Type III Sum of Squares	df	Mean Squares	F	Sig.
Corrected Model	38.356	7	5.497	8.683	.000
Intercept	52.101	1	52.101	82.558	.000
CG	15.173	2	7.587	12.021	.000
LG	.335	2	.167	.265	.768
CG LG	2.924	3	.975	1.544	.210
Error	46.700	74	.631		
Total	165.517	82			
Corrected total	85.057	81			

a R Squared =.451 (Adjusted R Squared =.399)

Note：CG = Cognition Group LG = Language Proficiency Group

5.5.1.8 Results：Effects of different levels of cognitive and linguistic ability on metaphor aptness

A similar 3 x 3 mixed-design ANOVA was carried out to further investigate to what extent the Chinese EFL learners with varying degrees of cognitive and linguistic ability differ with regard to aptness of the metaphor produced. The ANOVA analysis (Table 5.44) demonstrates that cognition had main effect (F (2, 82) = 15.561, p =.000) while language proficiency did not (F (2, 82) =.036, p =.965). In addition, the research found no significant two-way interaction between cognition and language proficiency (F (2, 82) = 2.365, p =.078).

Table 5.44 ANOVA Results with Between-subjects Factors, Cognition and Language Proficiency Group and Within-subjects Factor, Metaphor Aptness

Dependent variable：Aptness

Source	Type III Sum of Squares	df	Mean Squares	F	Sig.
Corrected Model	3558.934	7	508.419	12.229	.000
Intercept	3607.950	1	3607.950	86.785	.000
CG	1293.818	2	646.909	15.561	.000
LG	2.965	2	1.482	.036	.965
CG LG	294.991	3	98.330	2.365	.078
Error	3076.444	74	41.574		
Total	12291.000	82			
Corrected total	6635.378	81			

a R Squared =.536 (Adjusted R Squared =.492)

Note：CG = Cognition Group LG = Language Proficiency Group

5.5.1.9 Results: Effects of different levels of cognitive and linguistic ability on metaphor novelty

Likewise, a 3 x 3 mix-design ANOVA was performed to further examine to what extent the Chinese EFL learners with varying degrees of cognitive and linguistic ability differ with respect to the novelty of the metaphor produced. The analysis demonstrates a similar result as that made of metaphor aptness, i.e., cognition had main effect ($F\ (2, 82) = 10.583$, $p = .000$) while language proficiency did not ($F\ (2, 82) = .885$, $p = .417$). Besides, the research found a significant two-way interaction between cognition and language proficiency ($F\ (2, 82) = 4.710$, $p = .005$).

Table 5.45 ANOVA Results with Between-subjects Factors, Cognition and Language Proficiency Group and Within-subjects Factor, Metaphor Novelty

Dependent variable: Novelty

Source	Type III Sum of Squares	df	Mean Squares	F	Sig.
Corrected Model	427.684	7	61.098	12.767	.000
Intercept	223.197	1	223.197	46.641	.000
CG	101.287	2	50.644	10.583	.000
LG	8.471	2	4.236	.885	.417
CG LG	67.613	3	22.538	4.710	.005
Error	354.121	74	4.785		
Total	1126.000	82			
Corrected total	781.805	81			

a R Squared = .547 (Adjusted R Squared = .504)

Note: CG = Cognition Group LG = Language proficiency Group

5.5.2 Summary and discussion

5.5.2.1 Summary

The previous part discusses the problem that to what extent the Chinese EFL learners with varying degrees of cognitive and linguistic ability differ in their comprehension of the four types of metaphorical sentences and differ with respect to the density, aptness and novelty of the metaphor generated. The research has come up with several findings, which are summarized in the following.

1) The Chinese EFL learners with different cognitive ability differed significantly in their comprehension of the four types of metaphorical sentences.

2) The Chinese EFL learners' with varying levels of language proficiency differed significantly in their comprehension of the four types of metaphorical sentences.

3) The Chinese EFL learner varied in comprehension when they understood different types of metaphorical sentences.

4) Interactively, different levels of cognitive ability and language proficiency were found to make significant differences in the Chinese EFL learners' comprehension of the four types of metaphorical sentences.

5) The Chinese EFL learners with varying degrees of cognitive ability differed significantly in their comprehension of S 2 and S 3, but not in that of S1 and S4.

6) The Chinese EFL learners with varying degrees of language proficiency did not differ significantly in their comprehension of each type of metaphorical sentence.

7) Interactively, different levels of cognitive ability and language proficiency made significant differences in the Chinese EFL learners' comprehension of S3, but not that of the other

three types of metaphorical sentences.

8) The Chinese EFL learners' with varying degrees of cognitive ability differed significantly in their performances with respect to metaphor density, aptness and novelty while the learners with varying levels of language proficiency did not.

9) Interactively, different levels of cognitive ability and language proficiency made significant differences in the learners' performance with respect to metaphor novelty, but not that of density and aptness.

5.5.2.2 Discussion

Interestingly enough, the results reported in this experiment demonstrated that the Chinese EFL learners' with varying degrees of cognitive ability and language proficiency differed significantly in their comprehension of the four types of metaphorical sentences. This fact might suggest that when the learners are different in their cognitive ability and language proficiency, they have recourse to different cognitive and linguistic resources in order to understand the metaphorical sentences. In other words, when reading the metaphorical sentences, the learners who were more cognitively and linguistically competent might outperform those who were less competent, but not the reverse.

As far as the sentence type difference in metaphor comprehension is concerned, more complicated results emerged. The results indicated that, the Chinese EFL learners with varying degrees of cognitive ability and language proficiency did not differ in understanding S1 and S4. This means that when reading the sentences with the same conceptual metaphor and equivalent linguistic expression and the sentences containing words and expressions with similar literal meanings but different metaphorical meanings, the learners, no matter how different they were in cognitive ability and language proficiency, their comprehension did not vary significantly. Additionally, the learners with varying levels of cognitive ability differed significantly in understanding S2 and S3. This implies that when reading the sentences with the same conceptual metaphor but different linguistic expression and the sentences with different metaphors, the learners who were cognitively competent performed better than those who were less competent. However, differences in language proficiency did not make significant differences in the learners' comprehension of these two types of sentences. A feasible explanation for this fact might be attributed to the assumption that in understanding the metaphorical sentences, the Chinese EFL learners tended to make direct transfer of their knowledge of their first tongue to that of their target language. As a result, when the transfer was smooth, no matter how different they were in their cognitive ability and language proficiency, they did not differ significantly in their comprehension. However, when the transfer was not smooth, the cognitively competent learners would be more aware of the cultural differences in the two languages and/or would make more cognitive efforts in order to understand the sentences while the cognitive incompetent learners would not, or would be less conscious of the cultural differences and /or would make less cognitive efforts. And at this time, their language proficiency did not play significant roles. Therefore, the learners' differences in comprehension were more likely decided by the amount of cognitive efforts they put in.

As far as metaphor production is concerned, difference in cognitive ability was found to bring about difference in the Chinese EFL learners' performance of density, aptness and novelty of the metaphor produced. This means that in producing metaphors in the target language, the learners who were cognitively competent would tend to make more cognitive efforts consciously and/or would be more aware of the cultural differences in the languages concerned than those who were cognitively incompetent in order to produce more metaphors. In addition, they would make greater efforts to make the metaphors more apt and novel. On the contrary, the learners with varying degrees of language proficiency did not differ in their performances with respect to the three items (density, aptness and novelty) mentioned above. This once again suggested that metaphor production is more a matter of cognition rather than one of language proficiency. Very interestingly, a significant interaction was found between cognitive ability and language proficiency in the learners' performances with respect to novelty but not to density and aptness of the metaphors generated. A feasible explanation could be attributed to the assumption that although cognition was the decisive factor, the role of language proficiency could not be undervalued. In other words, on the one hand, supposing that the learners had already created metaphors in their minds, however, if they failed to find words that signified the concepts in their mental lexicon, they could thus not put the metaphors into words. On the other hand, the interaction was not found between cognition and language proficiency for the learners' performances with respect to density and aptness of the metaphors generated. Very likely, this was because, as the relevant test showed, many of the metaphors found in the learners' production protocols were the ones that were conventional. Alternatively, many learners were only aware of using metaphors they acquired in their production protocols. When they acquired these metaphors, they acquired both the concepts and the words. However, they were not so conscious and competent enough as to create new metaphors. Therefore, the interaction effect was not significant.

Notes

Assimilation and accommodation are two important terms in Piaget's cognitive psychology. Piaget used the term assimilation when he studies how children acquire knowledge. In his words, assimilation is the cognitive processing by which a person integrates new perceptual, or conceptual matter into existing schemata. Assimilation goes on all the time. Theoretically, it does not result in a change of schemata, but it does affect the growth of schemata and is thus a part of development. It is a part of the process by which the individual cognitively adapts to and organizes the environment. To Piaget, accommodation is the creation of new schemata or the modification of old schemata. By creating new schemata, the former cognitive structures are changed or developed to a certain degree. In Piaget's view, assimilation of stimulus goes on again after the accommodation of it. Both actions result in a change in, or development of cognitive structures. Piaget thinks that there will be generally a balance between these two cognitive processes which he calls equilibrium.

Chapter 6 Conclusion, Implication and Limitation

6.1 Introduction

The present research begins with a theoretical exploration of the question of whether metaphor learning for foreign language learners is cognitive or linguistic independently or both cognitive and linguistic, and then has tried to find evidence in support of the theoretical assumption with an experimental research. Moreover, the research, after the question has been answered, has investigated the roles played by cognition and language proficiency in the Chinese EFL learners' metaphor comprehension and production performances from different perspectives. This closing chapter begins with some general findings derived from the series of analyses carried out in the previous chapters. Then, the chapter will enter into discussions on the theoretical, methodological and pedagogical implications this research has for metaphor study from an applied linguistic perspective. Also included are the limitations and suggestions this study has for future research.

6.2 Major findings of the study

As stated in the preceding chapter, metaphor learning for the Chinese EFL learners comprises two aspects: metaphor comprehension and production, because the two are generally considered to be different cognitive processes. Consequently, the relevant findings are shown following these two lines.

1) Cognition and language proficiency were found to be closely correlated with the Chinese EFL learners' metaphor comprehension performance. More importantly, cognition and language proficiency have been found to have a significantly predictive power on the learners' metaphor comprehension performance. Specifically, cognition could explain 43.6% and language proficiency could do 43.9% of the variance in the learners' metaphor comprehension performance. This might suggest that metaphor comprehension for foreign language learners is both a cognitive and linguistic matter.

2) Cognition and language proficiency have been found to be significantly correlated with the Chinese EFL learners' metaphor production performance. Furthermore, cognition could account for a significant proportion of the variance of the learners' metaphor production performance (83.5%) whereas language proficiency does not. This might imply that metaphor production for foreign language learners is mainly a matter of cognition.

3) When the Chinese speaking learners were divided into higher and lower groups based on their cognitive level, cognition was found not to be a significant predictor of the variance of the metaphor comprehension performance of the lower groups (27.1%), but it was found to have a significant predictive power on the higher groups' metaphor comprehension performance (44.4%). Meanwhile, the research has found that language proficiency could explain a significant proportion of the variance of the metaphor comprehension performance of the lower group (48.3%) but not that of the higher group (6%). Regarding this, the research stated that cognition and language proficiency seemed to play different roles in the comprehension of metaphor when the learners were cognitively different. Specifically, cognition

appeared to have a more significant predictive power on the cognitively higher learners' metaphor comprehension and language proficiency seemed to play a more significant role in that of the cognitively poorer learners.

4) When the Chinese speaking learners were divided into higher and lower groups based on their cognitive level, the research found that cognition could consistently account for a significant proportion of the variance of the metaphor production performance of both the higher group (42.5%) and the lower one (58.8%). On the contrary, language proficiency's predictive power was not significant for the two groups' metaphor production performance. With respect to this finding, the research could conclude that metaphor production was fundamentally a matter of cognition no matter the learners were cognitively strong or weak.

5) Roughly similar findings were made of the metaphor comprehension and production performance when the learners were divided into the higher and lower groups based on their language proficiency level as those made when the learners were divided into two groups with cognition level as the criterion. The findings were roughly similar because the divisions made based on cognitive and linguistic levels were not significantly marked. Namely, the learners who were cognitively stronger were very likely those who were also linguistically stronger, and vice versa. However, the only exception was found about the role played by cognition in the metaphor comprehension performance of the cognitively poorer learners and that of the linguistically poorer ones. Specifically, for the metaphor comprehension performance of the cognitively weaker learners, cognition was not found to be a significant predictor of their comprehension performance while it was a significant one of that of the linguistically poorer ones. The finding thus suggests that when the learners were cognitively

poor, they were very likely to seek more help from their linguistic knowledge in order to understand the metaphorical sentences because it could still explain 27.1% of the variance of metaphor comprehension although it was not significant.

6) Language proficiency has been consistently found to have a significantly predictive power on the comprehension performance of each type of metaphorical sentences while cognition can account for a significant proportion of the variance of the comprehension performance of S2, S3 and S4 except S1. When the metaphorical sentences are both conceptually and linguistically equivalent in the source language and the target language, only language proficiency is the significant predictor of the variance of metaphor comprehension performance while both language proficiency and cognition can be significant predictors when the sentences are the ones (1) with same conceptual metaphor but different linguistic expression, (2) with different conceptual metaphors, and (3) whose words and expressions have similar literal meanings but different metaphorical meanings. In addition, cognition was consistently found to explain a significant proportion of the variance of the learners' performance with respect to density, aptness and novelty of the metaphor generated whereas language proficiency was invariably not.

7) The Chinese EFL learners' with varying degrees of cognitive ability and language proficiency differ significantly in their comprehension performance of the four types of metaphorical sentences.

8) The Chinese EFL learners with varying degrees of cognitive ability differ significantly in their comprehension of S2 and S3, but not in that of S1 and S4.

9) The Chinese EFL learners with varying degrees of language proficiency do not differ significantly in their

comprehension of each type of metaphorical sentences.

10) The Chinese EFL learners with varying levels of cognitive ability differ significantly in their performance with respect to the density, aptness and novelty of the metaphors generated whereas those with different levels of language proficiency did not vary significantly.

6.3 Implications

6.3.1 Theoretical implications

As was discussed in Chapter 1 and 2, metaphor study attracts the attention of researchers from a constellation of disciplines where different theories are provided. However, just as Gibbs (2001: 36) pointed out, no single theory of metaphor presently available will account for all of the different kinds of metaphor, nor perhaps will any one theory be able to do so in the future. However, according to Reynolds & Ortony (1980: 1110), in the long history of language teaching, generally speaking, metaphor teaching has been carried out with one or more of a variety of difficulties that frequently relate to the inadequacy of the underlying theoretical account of metaphor *per se*. Therefore, an applied linguistic study of metaphor like the present one should have a good eye for the following points. Otherwise, it will fail to reveal the real nature of how learners, especially foreign language learners, pick up the target language.

First of all, applied linguistics researchers who are interested in metaphor should be well aware of the origins of different definitions and descriptions of metaphor in order to construct a theoretically-sound basis (Cameron & Low 1999). For example, on the one hand, if metaphor is regarded as purely linguistic or rhetorical as what Aristotle was mistaken to be, the cognitive base of metaphor will be likely overlooked. On the other hand, if too much emphasis is given to the cognitive concern of metaphor, it will result in insufficient attention paid to variations on the grammatical/linguistic form of metaphor that carry significance in discourse (Picken 2001: 64). What is more, it will divert teachers and students' attention not to the metaphors in everyday conversations and writings but in poetry or drama, which, Lakoff (1998) believes, are the main sources of metaphors in the traditional theory. Just as Cameron & Low (1999: 81) argue, because of the powerful influence of cognitive linguistics, more researches from applied linguistics approach tend to emphasize metaphor's cognitive and cultural roles, downplaying the linguistic, in the reaction to what was seen as over-emphasis on the literary and stylistic functions of metaphor.

Secondly, an applied linguistic study of metaphor should clearly distinguish between the contexts where the study is conducted. This is crucially important because language learning and teaching in different context is rather different and metaphor is quite a culture-specific phenomenon. On the one hand, as Ellis (1994: 11) states, the L1 terms signal a characteristic of level of proficiency in the language, suggesting an intuitive, "native-like", "full", or "perfect" command of the language while the concept of L2 (non-native language, second language, foreign language) may indicate a lower level of proficiency in the language in comparison with the primary language and imply the prior availability to the individual of a L1. On the other hand, although metaphor is a universal cognitive mechanism as Lakoff & Johnson (1980) argue, people in different cultures may vary from one another in their specific views about certain things in the world (Yu 1998; 2003; Charteris-Black 2002). For instance, a metaphor study in the L1 context may not give priority to factors such the learners' language proficiency or culture problems. On the contrary, these factors should become the main focus of a similar study in the L2 context because L2 learners can not be expected to approach figurative speech the way native speakers do because of their different linguistic and cultural experience (Kecskes 2006: 227; Cooper 1999). To sum up, an applied linguistic study of metaphor, especially one like the present research which is conducted in a foreign language context, should be well aware of the aforementioned differences.

Thirdly, metaphor researchers in applied linguistics should be expected to give their attention not only to metaphor learning in general but also to that at different stages, cognitive or linguistic or others. For example, when the present research studied the roles of cognition and language proficiency in the metaphor comprehension and production performance of the Chinese EFL learners with varying cognitive and linguistic ability, the results turned out to be varied and slightly different from those when the learners were taken as a whole. In other words, metaphor performance may to some extent vary from learners to learners because they have different characteristics which in turn may affect the metaphor learning process and outcome.

Fourthly, to study metaphor learning, one should give due and equal consideration to both metaphor comprehension and production. As is reviewed in Chapter 3, many relevant studies to date have been interested mainly in metaphor comprehension, with comparatively less sufficient attention given to metaphor production. As a consequence, only part of the picture is displayed while another part is left relatively unclearly exposed. The present research calls for a change so as to reveal the whole picture of metaphor learning, which in turn may provide more valuable suggestions to greatly and comprehensively develop language learners' metaphoric competence. Furthermore, for researchers who are interested in foreign language learners' acquisition of metaphor, how to design the comprehension test and to evaluate the production performance remain crucially important. The models developed by Deignan *et al* (1997) and Charteris-Black (2002), as were used in the present research, are believed to be suitable to test foreign language learners' metaphor comprehension because similarities and differences in the concepts and linguistic expressions of the source and target language are taken into account. With reference to the evaluation of metaphor production performance, a multi-dimensional method was used, i. e., metaphor was evaluated in terms of density, aptness and novelty instead of using one as the criterion, which is believed to comprehensively and objectively measure the real nature of metaphor production performance. Therefore, these methods are considered to be useful for relevant similar research in the future.

6.3.2 Pedagogical implications

A very fundamental task for researchers in applied linguistics is to seek optimal ways to facilitate the processes of language learning in general (Yang Yonglin 2002a: 114). Since the present research is concerned about the roles the Chinese EFL learners' cognitive and linguistic ability play in their English metaphor comprehension and production performances, it may have some implications for language, especially foreign language teaching and learning.

Firstly, it is advisable that Chinese EFL teachers and learners broaden and deepen their understanding of the real nature of metaphor in order to guide them in their teaching and learning activities. As is discussed in Chapter 2, due to various reasons, metaphor to many, if not all, people, is just a figure of speech which is used to make speech or writing vivid, and it is mainly found in literary and poetic writings. Accordingly, metaphor can only be thought of negatively as a manipulation of, a departure from, or an addition to the literal (Cameron & Low 1999: 78). Metaphors are still felt by some to be largely literary and thus recondite, obscure, and difficult partially because they are often hard to treat in a clear, rule-governed way (Littlemore and Low 2006: 269). This limited knowledge of metaphor deflects teachers and learners' attention away from the centrality of metaphor in language (Jiang Yajun 2002). Fortunately, with the rise of cognitive linguistics, the cognitive nature of metaphor is revealed. Metaphor is thus seen as a cognitive mechanism by which people know one thing in terms of another. In fact, metaphors have been used in teaching since Plato as way of making unfamiliar concepts familiar (Fain 2001: 39). Moreover, metaphor is considered to be pervasive in language, not just in poetics and drama. More importantly, metaphor, according to Fainsilber & Ortony (1987: 240-241), can fulfill the necessary communication function of conveying continuous experiential information using a discrete symbol system. They formulated three hypotheses (inexpressibility, compactness and vividness) whose functions are believed to facilitate learning. The first is that metaphor can make possible the expression of ideas that may be difficult or impossible to express using literal language. This is because certain aspects of natural experience are never encoded in language and metaphor carry with them the extra meanings never encoded in language. The sentence "*The thought slipped my mind like a squirrel behind a tree*" is cited as an example to explain that the characteristics of squirrels slipping behind trees (swiftness, suddenness, ungraspableness) are difficult to express using literal language. The second is that metaphor can express ideas compactly in the sense that metaphors help to convey "chunks" of information rather than discrete units. This is so because language partitions the continuity of experience into discrete units comprised of words and phrases having a relatively narrow referential range. The third is that metaphor, perhaps through imagery, can provide a vivid and, therefore, memorable and emotion-arousing representation of perceived experience. What is more, in studying metaphor as communication, Sticht (1998: 622) thinks that metaphor can serve as linguistic tools for overcoming certain cognitive limitations, arguing that metaphor functions as a tool to extend the capacity of active memory using medium of speech in communication. To sum up, if Chinese EFL learners and teachers are well aware of these functions of metaphor, their teaching and learning will be much enhanced.

Secondly, since the present research found that the Chinese EFL learners' metaphor comprehension and production were greatly attributable to their cognitive and linguistic ability, perhaps foreign language teachers are expected to commit themselves to improving learners' abilities in these two aspects in order to enhance their proficiency in metaphorical language. The results of the present study seem to imply that priority should go to the training of learners' cognitive ability. The reasons for this appear to be two-folded. In the first place, metaphor is fundamentally cognitive. Therefore, the key to enhancing learners' metaphoric competence should depend considerably on whether or not they are well trained cognitively. In the second place, linguistic ability has been always a major concern of language teaching, so much progress has been achieved in this respect although it can not be said to have been optimized. For improving learners' cognitive ability, teachers should be advised to carefully design some exercises aimed at stimulating cognitive activities in order to exploit learners' innate cognitive drive to make sense of their environment (Paul 1998: 1). Since L2 learners, especially those who have studied the L2 in an instructional environment, are usually much more familiar with the literal meanings of the lexical unit than with their figurative meanings and languages may have much lexical equivalency at the literal level but much less at the metaphorical, figurative level (Kecskes 2006: 227), metaphorical language teaching should be organized to contrast the lexical items in terms of the conceptual domains they reflect rather than contrast verbal structures on their own (Danesi 1994: 461). That might be why some researchers called for explicit instruction in the conceptual system of the target language especially when it is different from that of the source language (Johnson 1996). Teaching concepts rather than just linguistic expressions by providing learners with a picture of a set of underlying concepts that motivate a number of frequently occurring figurative units is believed to be helpful for second language learners to master figurative language with less time than that is normally required when they are provided with a picture of a set of underlying concepts that motivate a number of frequently occurring figurative units, which, in turn, will facilitate and strengthen the acquisition of the linguistic items (Charteris-Black 2002: 107, 109). Since concept teaching is considered to be important to cultivate learners' cognitive ability, which will ultimately enhance their metaphoric competence, to work towards the goal, the Chinese speaking teachers of English should take a few things into consideration: 1) It is necessary to work out a conceptually-based syllabus which should connect the verbal categories to be learned with their related conceptual domains. The syllabus is to be organized to simply identify and catalogue the *vehicles* that underlie specific *topics*, which should be integrated with grammatical and communicative syllabi (Danesi 1994: 459-462). 2) Metaphorical language should be given more emphasis in textbook-compiling. Metaphorical language should no longer be presented as exceptions to the rule in the first-level textbooks and that work on it should not be left only to courses on literature (Ponterotto 1994). 3) Since metaphoric competence has an important role to play in all aspects of communicative competence, metaphorical language should hold a position in the testing from the earliest to the most advanced stages of learning (Littlemore & Low 2006). 4) It is necessary to encourage foreign language learners' metaphoric awareness because an enhanced awareness on the part of the language learners can help them effectively master metaphorical language and their retention of novel figurative expression (Boers 2000a; 2000b; Low 1998). Conscious reflection on the metaphorical nature of language and comparisons between L1 and L2 should be encouraged in order to raise learners' awareness (Deignan *et al* 1997; Paul 1998).

Thirdly, it is advisable that Chinese EFL teachers should encourage learners to make active use of their creativity in order to create novel metaphors and understand metaphors which have no equivalent concepts in their native language. This is emphasized here because the present research, in testing the subjects' ability to understand the different types of metaphorical sentence and in measuring the novelty of the metaphors they generated, found that many subjects gave very disappointing performances in their understanding of the metaphorical sentences whose concepts are not equivalent to those of their native language and achieved much low scores in producing novel metaphors. As is known, creativity is defined as the ability to produce many different ideas in response to a problem and is believed to be present in everyone and it varies from person to person in level (Albert & Kormos 2004: 280). More importantly, relevant research shows that there exists a strong positive relationship between metaphoric thinking and creativity (Glicksohn *et al* 1993) and that learners with high creativity tend to use more metaphors and produce more novel metaphors than those with low creativity in their performance Fine & Lockwood (1986). Therefore, if a more urgent aim of education is to prepare qualified labor force or citizens for the twenty-first century, then Chinese EFL teachers should foresee the correlation between learners' metaphoric competence and creativity. More practically, language learners should be well prepared in both language and thinking for the society with increasing intercultural communication and the labor marketing needed in the twenty-first century of China.

6.3.3 Methodological implications

Methodologically, this study adopted an experimental research model to investigate the roles played by the cognitive ability and linguistic ability of the Chinese EFL learners in their metaphor comprehension and production performances. By using a research design like this, the study has some methodological implications for metaphor research in future.

Firstly, a stratificational analytical method was adopted to examine the roles of the Chinese EFL learners' cognitive and linguistic abilities in their metaphor comprehension and production performances. Specifically, the research first employed an analysis of the roles of the two independent variables in the learners' general scores of metaphor comprehension and production performances without dividing the subjects into high and low groups according to their cognitive and linguistic levels and without separating the learners' general performance into that of each component part of the tests. Then, the analysis was made of the relationships between the learners' cognitive and linguistic abilities and their performances when the learners were divided on their cognitive and linguistic levels respectively. After completion of these two kinds of analysis, the researcher also conducted one which aimed at examining the relationships between the two factors and the learners' performances in each component part of the tests (i.e., each of the four types of metaphorical sentences and density, aptness and novelty with reference to which metaphor is measured). Finally, the ANOVA analyses were performed to investigate the main and interactive effects of the two variables in order to reveal what factors are involved and how these factors are interacting with each other in the learners' metaphor comprehension and production. This stratificational analytical method has provided a comprehensive picture of the relationships existing among the learners' cognitive and linguistic abilities and their metaphor comprehension and production.

Secondly, spontaneous elicitation method was taken to collect data. Other methods such translation, interview, judgment, sentence stem or even multiple choice questions were not chosen because they, as were discussed in Chapter 3, were not unproblematic. Using this method, the research collected the naturally occurring data which could ensure the validity of the tests

Thirdly, the research measured the learners' metaphor production performance in terms of density, aptness and novelty. This was very likely to be a more comprehensive way to test learners' ability in metaphor production, which has not yet been found to be used in relevant studies.

6.3.4 Limitations

Needless to say, the present study only offers a tiny part of a huge iceberg in the research on the roles played by cognition and language proficiency in the Chinese EFL learners' metaphor comprehension and production performances. Moreover, due to some objective and subjective limitations, the present research is far from perfect and much work has to be done if a complete picture of the Chinese EFL learners' metaphor comprehension and production processes is presented. Specifically, this research has some limitations, which are exposed in the following.

Firstly, the between-group difference in the sample is small. As is shown in the previous analyses, the present research divided the subjects into different groups according to their levels of cognition and language proficiency in order to see how their cognitive and linguistic abilities affected their metaphor comprehension and production performances. But all the subjects were college English majors who differed slightly. In other words, although the subjects were from four different classes ranging from grade three to grade four, the second group lagged behind the first by only about half a year. Therefore, differences in cognition and language proficiency vary little accordingly. Taken this into account, the research findings should be interpreted with caution when the analyses were made of the different groups as were divided by levels of cognition and language proficiency.

Secondly, the overall statistical sample is relatively small. In the present research, only English majors were chosen to participate in the series of tests in order to examine the relationships between cognition and language proficiency and metaphor comprehension and production. This kind of sampling limits the findings and makes it difficult to generalize them. In other words, it should be cautious to apply the findings to explaining the relevant issues that lie for non-English majors' metaphor comprehension and production performances.

Thirdly, the conceptualization of cognitive ability and language proficiency should be further modified in order to make them more closely related to the research. In terms of the conceptualization of cognitive ability, the present research formulated only thirty questions. Although the research designed the questionnaire with reference to the ones previously adopted by the relevant studies and got a test result with a highly significant reliability coefficient, the number of the questions included is still relatively small. With regard to the conceptualization of language proficiency, the present study took TEM 4 as the criterion. As is known, this examination includes some items such as dictation as one component, which might not be related to metaphor comprehension and production. Therefore, the two conceptualizations need to be modified in order to make them more relevant to metaphor research.

6.3.5 Suggestions for future research

Applied linguistic study of metaphor learning, especially in foreign language context, remains a relatively unexplored terrain. The present research provides some interesting findings with respect to the roles played by cognition and language proficiency in determining the Chinese EFL learners' metaphor comprehension and production performances. The research described in this book needs to be both broadened and deepened in the following ways.

Firstly, additional studies should aim at examining the possible roles played by other factors such as learners' cognitive style, motivation, creativity, sex, age, etc., in the Chinese EFL learners' metaphor comprehension and production. More importantly, how these factors combine with cognition and language proficiency, the two primary ones, to affect the learners' metaphor learning is another area worth further investigation. For example, motivation is regarded as a crucial factor to affect the degree of effort learners are prepared to make in order to understand metaphors (Littlemore 2001c: 346). Relevant studies might also explore how these factors coupled with context or familiarity of metaphor affect foreign language learners' metaphor processing. In this research, for example, presented to the subjects are mainly the metaphors which are unfamiliar and in non-supportive contexts. Presenting the metaphors in supportive contexts to see which factors would affect or what strategies learners would frequently adopt might lend a different perspective on how the foreign language learners deal with metaphorical expressions. Such multi-dimensional studies are needed because foreign language metaphor learning is undoubtedly a rather complex cognitive process which is believed to be decided by many rather than by one or only some factors without interference of others.

Secondly, a replication of an identical experiment should be performed by Chinese college students who come from different types of colleges or universities and have different majors because a large-scale survey of the qualities of English-major students in China shows that English majors who have been enrolled in English departments of several foreign languages institutes form a special body of their own and are different in various ways from their peer students in other types of universities (Yang Yonglin 2002a).

Thirdly, other studies should be administered to Chinese EFL learners who are apparently at different levels of English learning stages, such as middle school students, first year college students and/or postgraduates in order to investigate how much weight learners' factors such as mentioned above affected the development of their metaphor comprehension and production performances. To sum up, how these factors affect the metaphor comprehension and production of primary, intermediate and advanced learners of foreign language.

Another issue that needs to be addressed is that of a comparison between the roles played by the aforementioned factors affect both of their Chinese and English metaphor comprehension and production performances. Rephrasingly, future studies should be conducted to investigate whether and more importantly how these factors exert similar or different effects on language learners' L1 and L2 metaphor comprehension and production performances.

Appendixes

Appendix I The Advanced Raven Intelligence Test

瑞文高级推理测试

北京师范大学辅仁应用心理发展中心

姓名________ 性别________ 出生年月____年____月____日
测验日期________ 年龄____岁____月____
学校________年级________班级________

说明：

各位同学，感谢你们参加此次测试活动。以下是一套高级推理测试练习，每页有两组图形，上方的大框格内应有九个小图形按照一定的规律排列，其中一个被删除掉了的，请你通过研究图形的规律，并从下面所给的八个小图形中选择一个填到大框格内空格里使其符合原来的规律，你只要把选准的图形的标号填到上面的空格中就行了，不需要你画图。

共有 36 道试题，希望在 45 分钟内做完。你不要放弃每道题的练习机会。在做题的过程中对不会的以及没有把握的试题，不要做猜测。

Note

（Note that all the thirty-six questions were originally presented to the subjects with each question printed on a piece of

A4 paper. That is，originally，the test is composed of thirty six pages. For the sake of space limitation，they are condensed here into twelve pages. Therefore，the figures arranged here are not in the form that was used in the formal test.)

1.

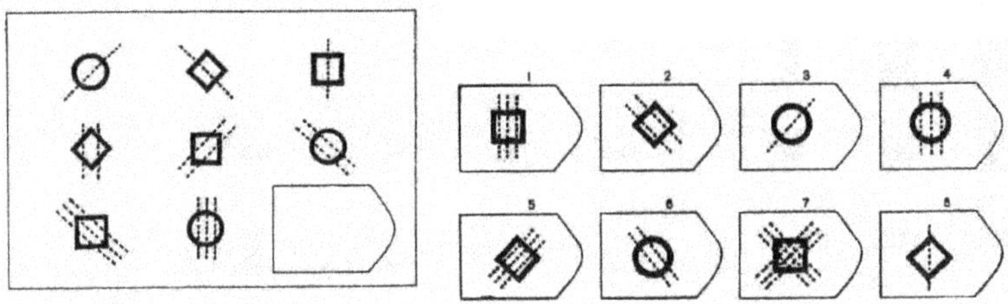

2.

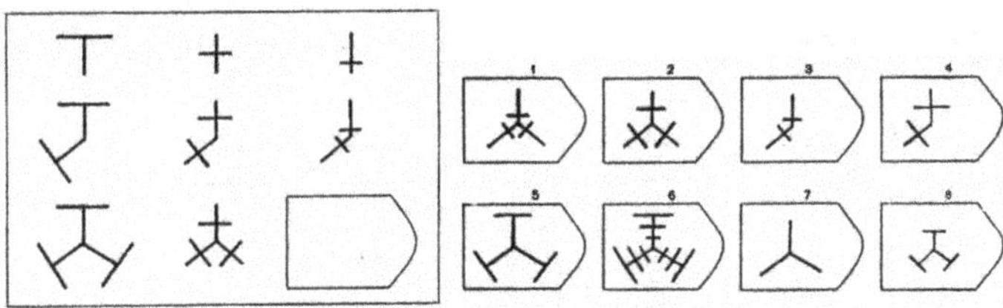

3.

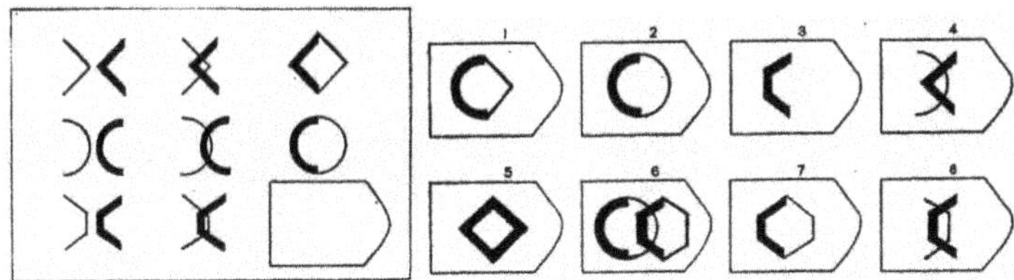

4.

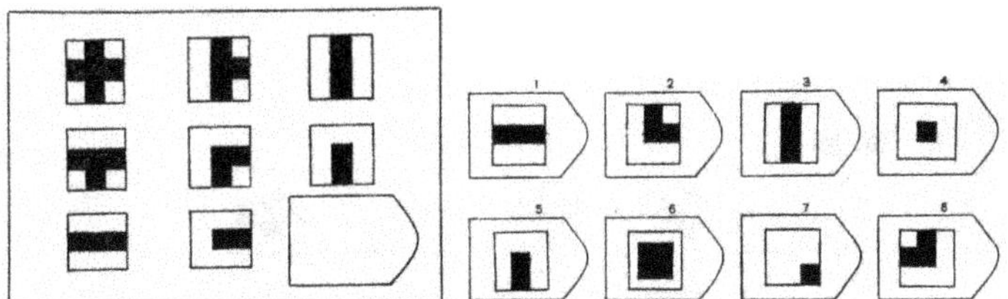

5.

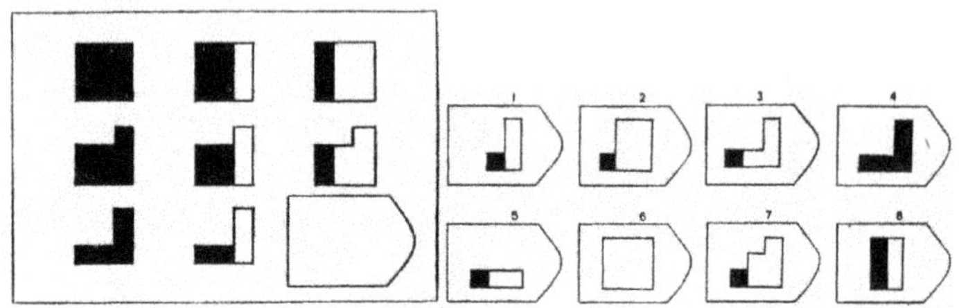

6.

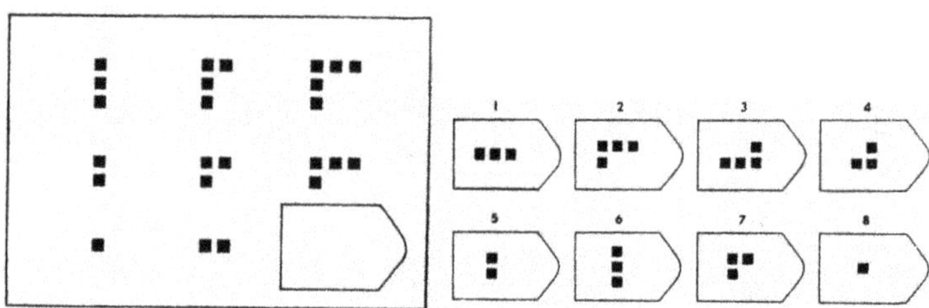

7.

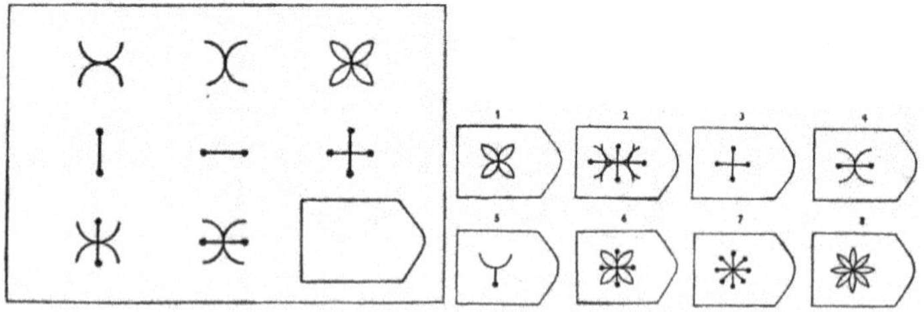

8.

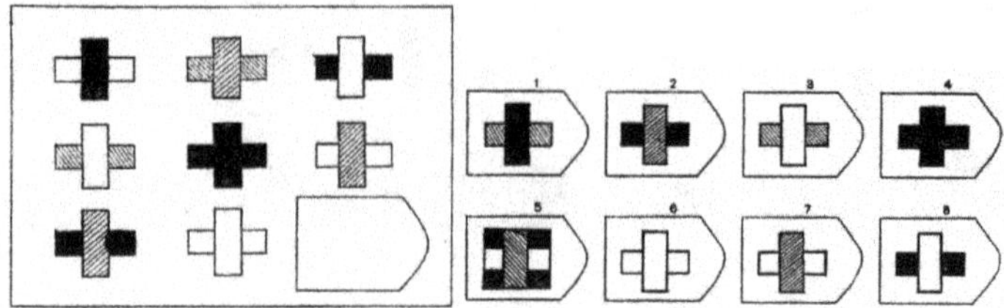

9.

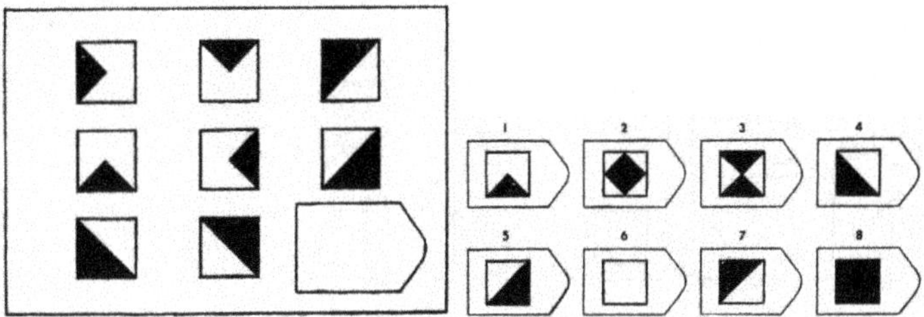

10.

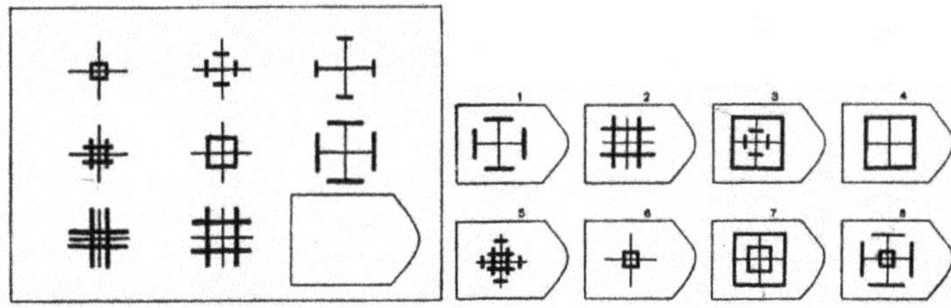

11.

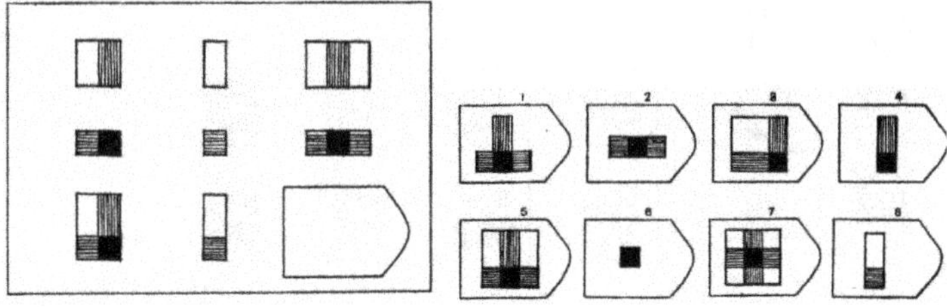

12.

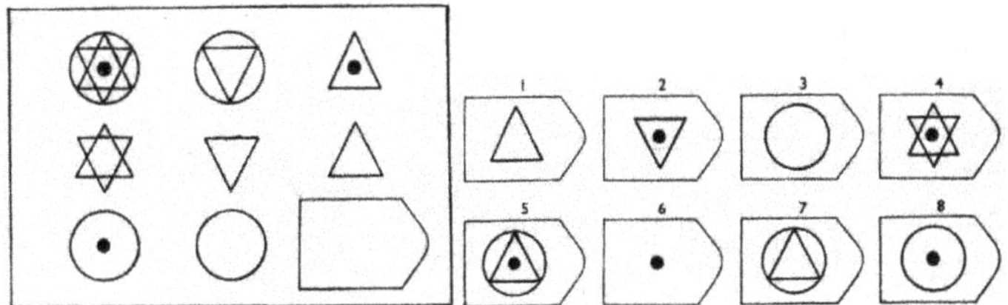

13.

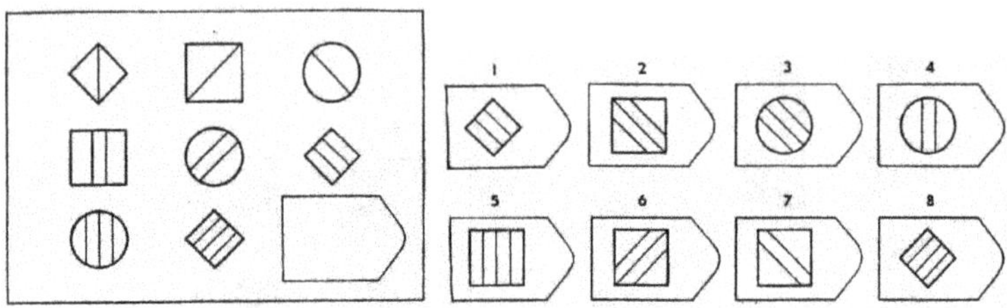

14.

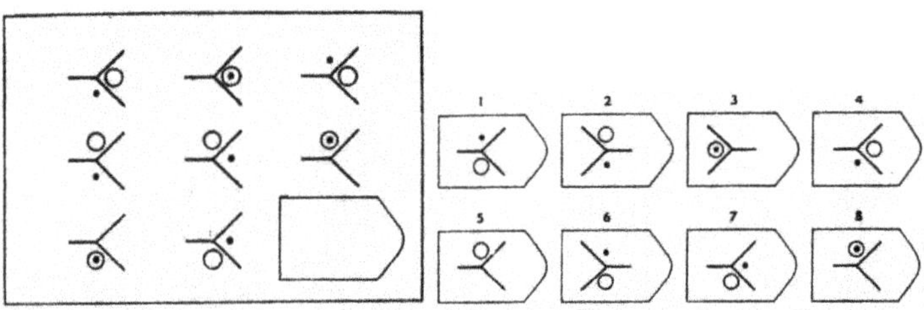

15.

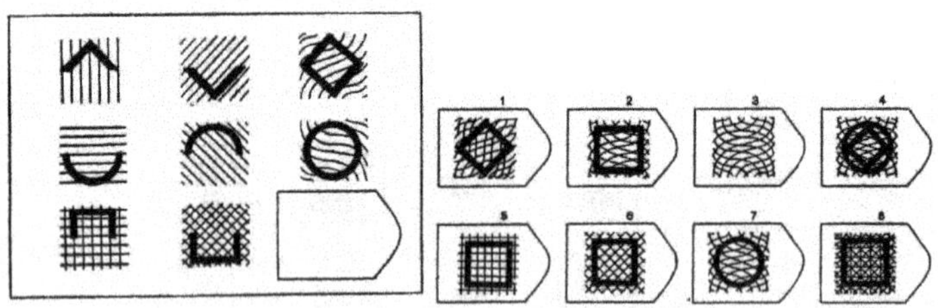

16.

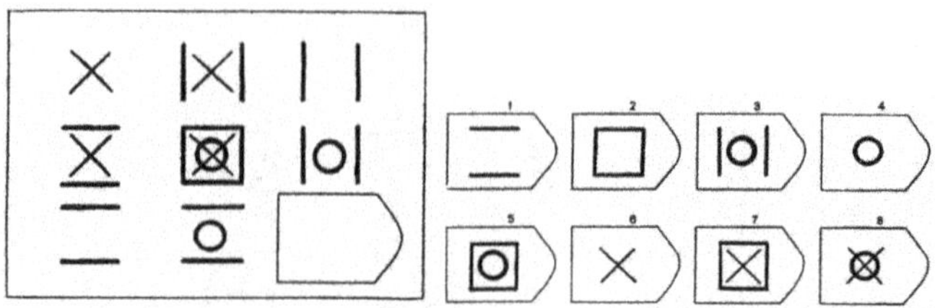

17.

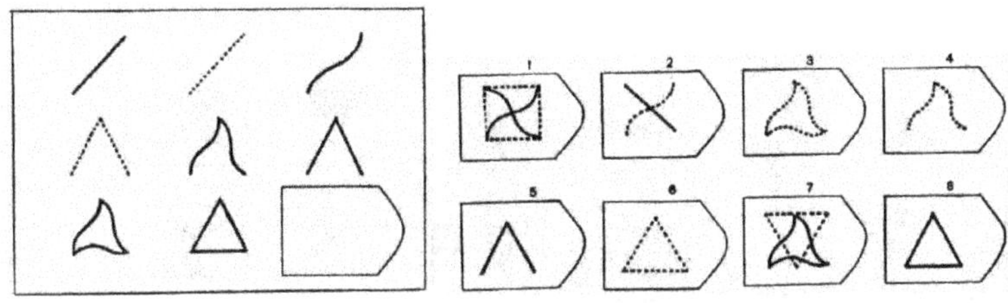

18.

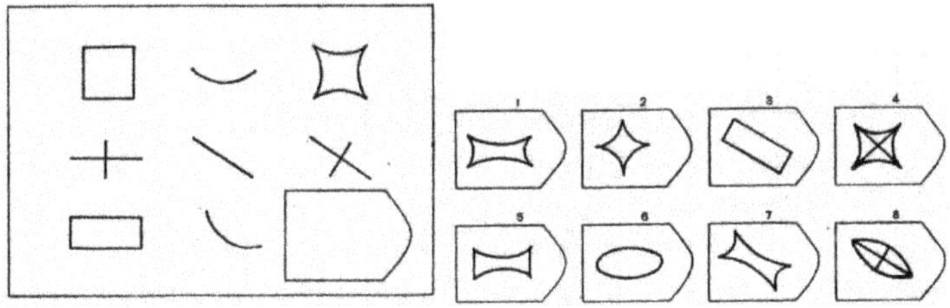

19.

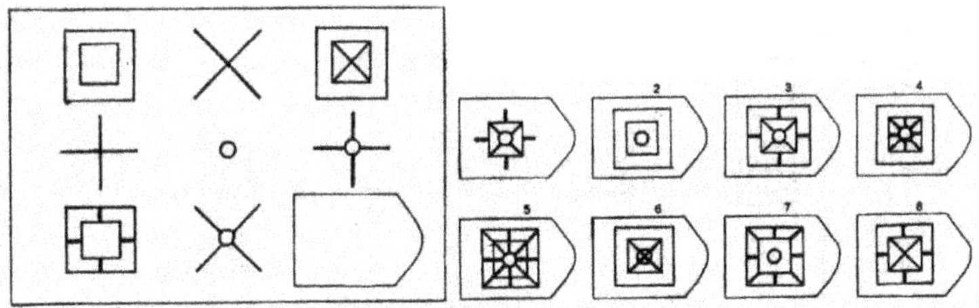

20.

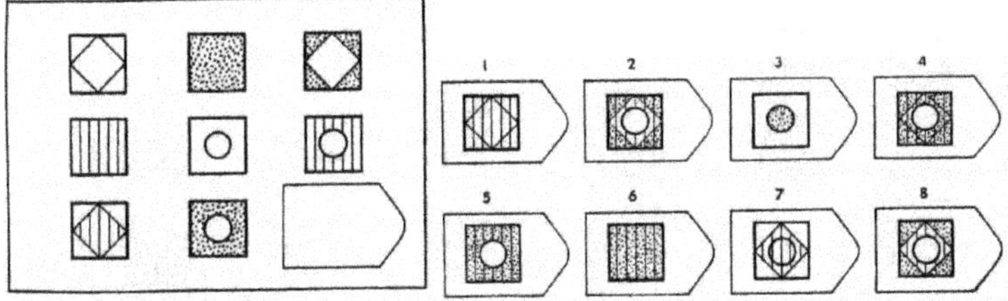

21.

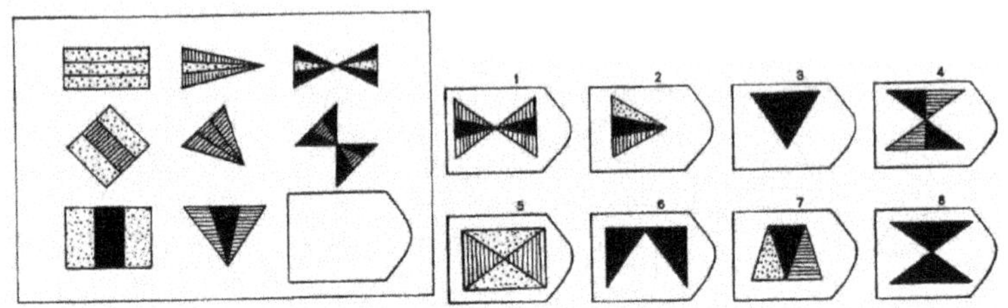

22.

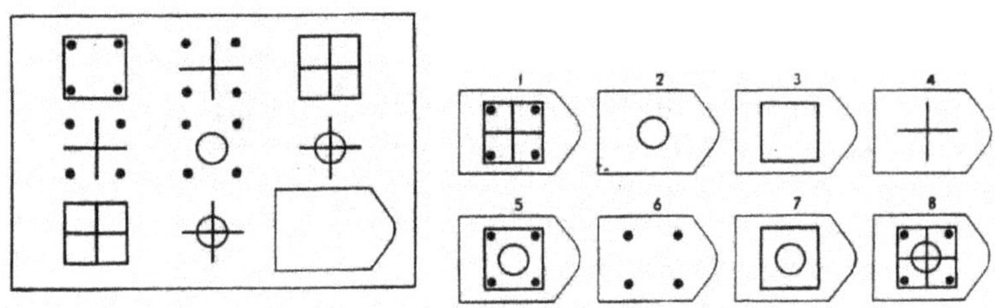

23.

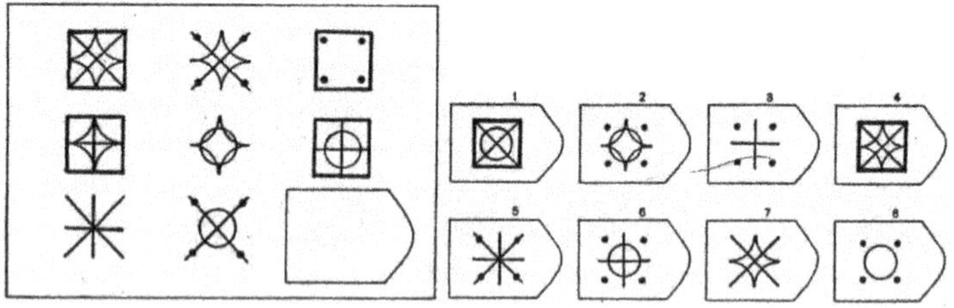

24.

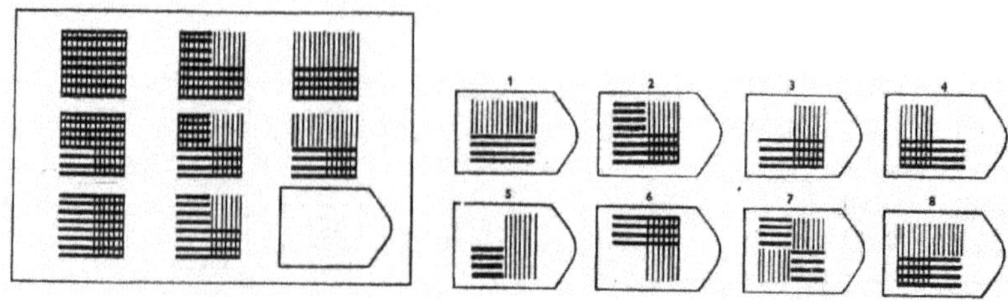

25.

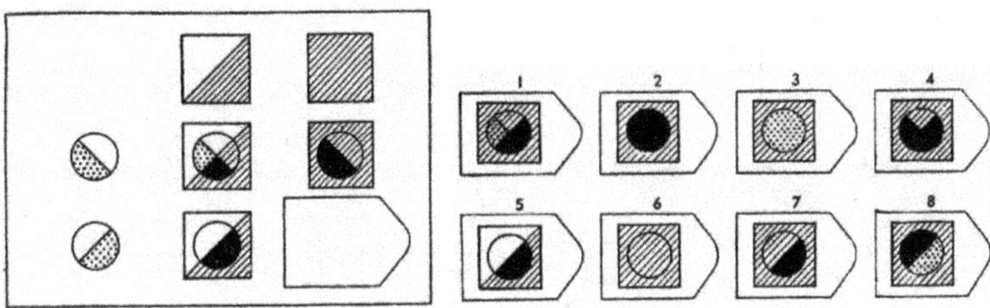

26.

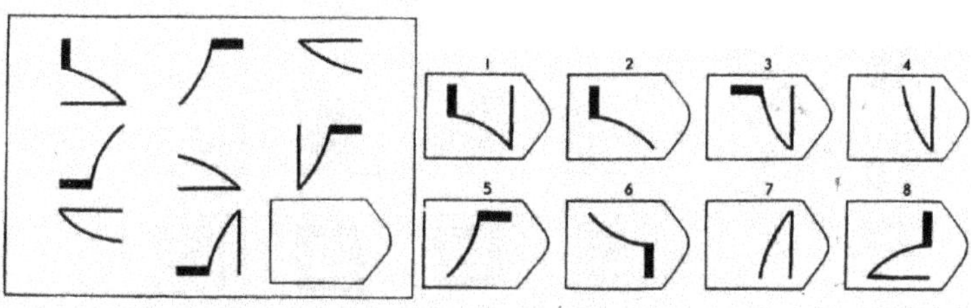

27.

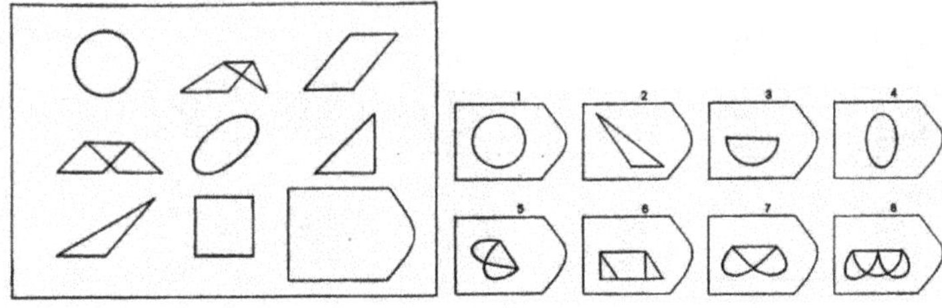

28.

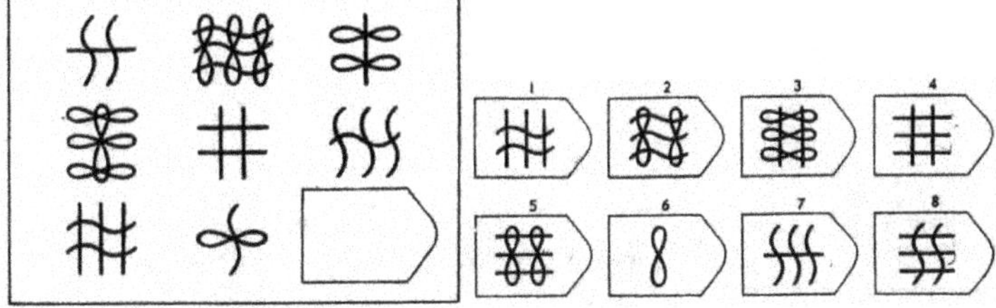

29.

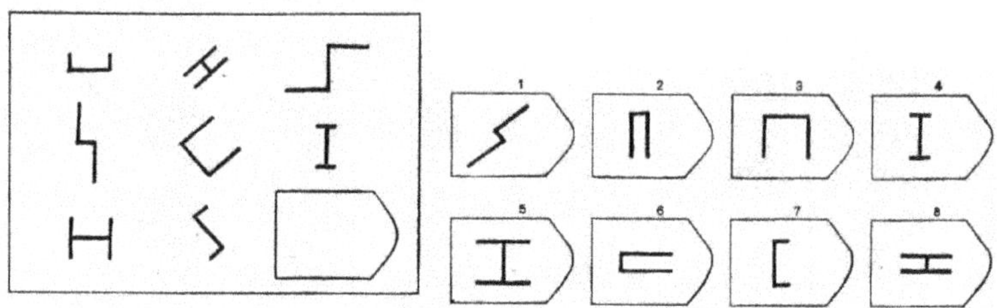

30.

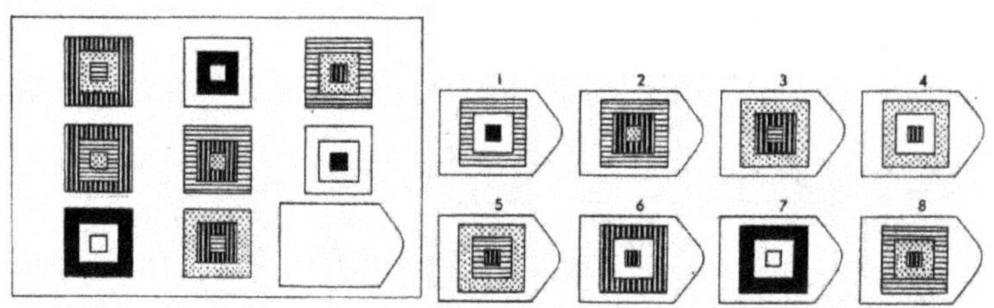

31.

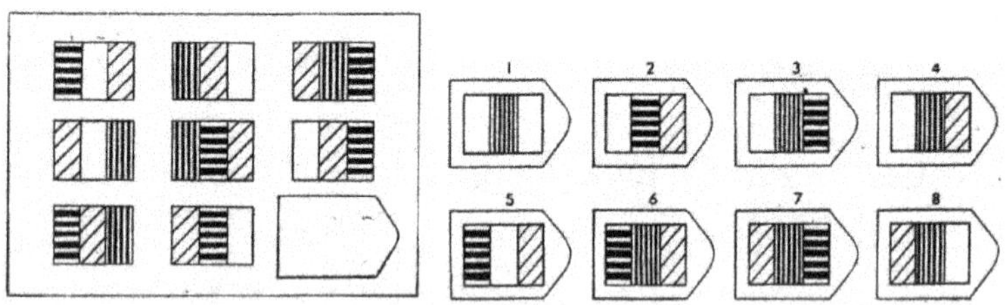

32.

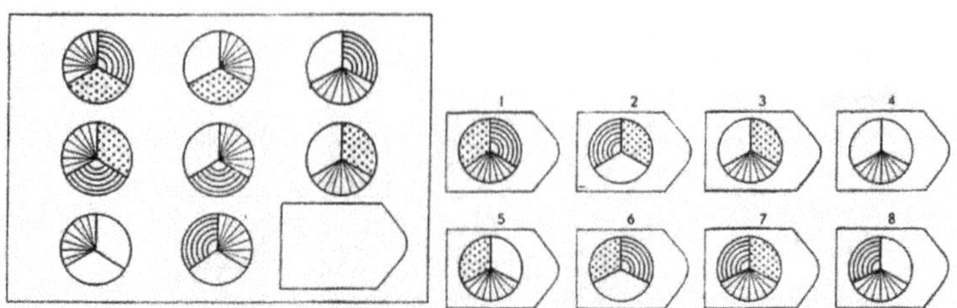

33.

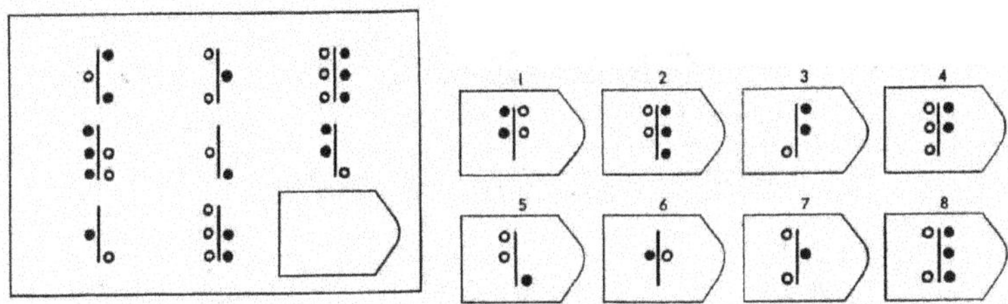

34.

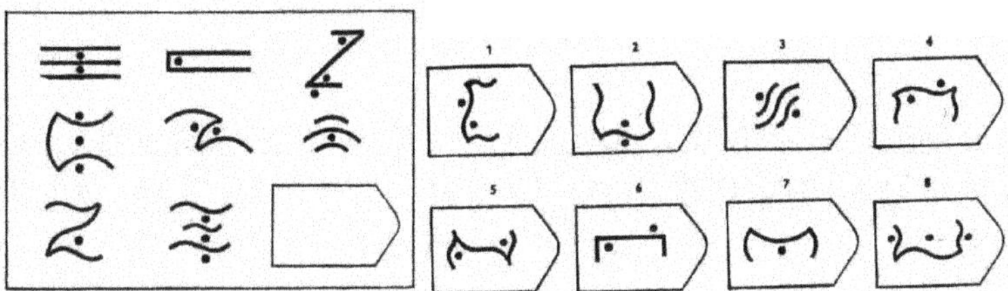

35.

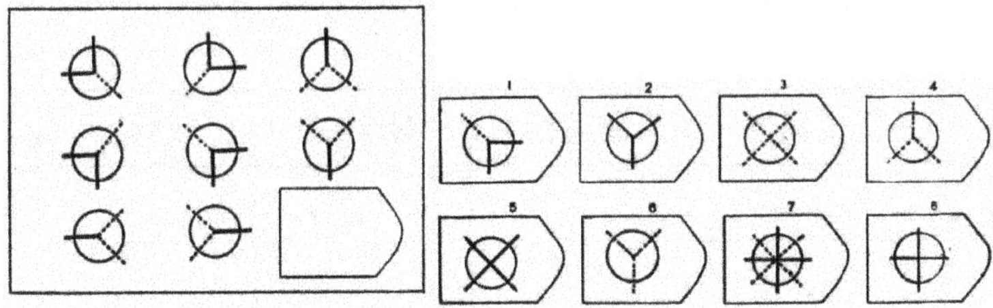

36.

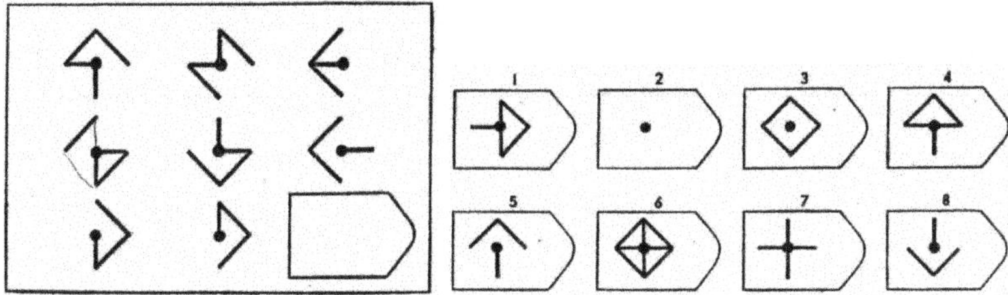

Appendix II The Creative Thinking Test

创造性思维测试

北京师范大学辅仁应用心理发展中心

姓名________ 性别________出生年月日____年____月____日
测验日期________ 年龄________岁________月________
学校________年级________班级________

说明：

这套创造性思维练习可以增进你的想象力，开拓你的思维，并提高你的思维能力，希望你保持轻松愉快的心情以尽可能快的速度来完成练习。

全套练习希望在50分钟内做完。请不要放弃每道题的练习机会。第一道题要求在规定的时间交上来，其余各题不分别限定时间。希望你不要提前交卷，因为你多想一想还会得出更多更好的答案。

计分：

	流畅性	变通性	独创性	总计
一				
二				
三				
四				
五				

一、词语联想(2 分钟一小题)

1	2	3	4	5	6	7	8	9	10

二、故事标题

下面有两个有趣的故事，可是它们没有标题。你仔细看完故事后，给这两个故事分别想几个恰当的标题。标题的数目越多，越切合故事，越生动、有趣、新颖、越好。

故事一

标题：____

一天，山上的一只猴子下山找吃的东西，它看到一块玉米地，便走进地里掰了一个玉米棒子扛在肩上，高兴地往前走。

它又走进了一片桃园，看见桃子沉甸甸地挂在树上。它想，桃子比玉米好吃，于是丢掉玉米，上树摘桃。它摘了一大把桃子，便赶路去了。

它又来到一片西瓜地。地里有好多又大又圆的西瓜。猴子把桃子全部扔掉，摘了一个最大的西瓜。天色已晚，猴子决计抱着西瓜回家。

在上山时，猴子遇见一只兔子。这只兔子在他面前欢快地蹦跳着，样子很可爱。猴子马上扔下西瓜，去追兔子。兔子钻进树丛，一会就不见了。猴子只好空手回家。

故事二

标题：____

夏天的一个周末，所有的市内火车都很挤。一个老人上了火车，想找一个座位。他发现有一个座位上没人，但座位上有一个手提包。他问旁边的一位穿戴讲究的青年：

“这个位子有人吗？”

“有人，他买报纸去了。”

“我先坐一会儿，等他回来了再让他吧。”老人说着就坐下了。

十分钟后，火车开了。

“哎呀，他误车了。”老人说，“他的包还留在车上呢！”老人说着就抓住提包，想把包从窗口扔到月台上去。

这个穿戴讲究的青年急忙跳起来阻止老人：

“别扔，这是我的包！”

三、小设计

公园的一大块不平地上要建 7 个亭子，请你设计建亭子及道路的分布图样，使亭子的布局和道路的安排既美观又实用。亭子用小圆圈表示，道路用单线表示。发挥你的想象力，设计尽可能多的图样。在下面的每一个大方格内画一个设计图样。能想多少就想多少，剩下方格不画也可以。

四、在椭圆上补画

请你以每一个椭圆为基础，添补出各种不同的东西来！不要求画得十分仔细、十分好，但要求别人一看就明白你画的是什么(不能用文字说明)。画的东西越多越独出心裁越好。剩下椭圆不补画也可以。

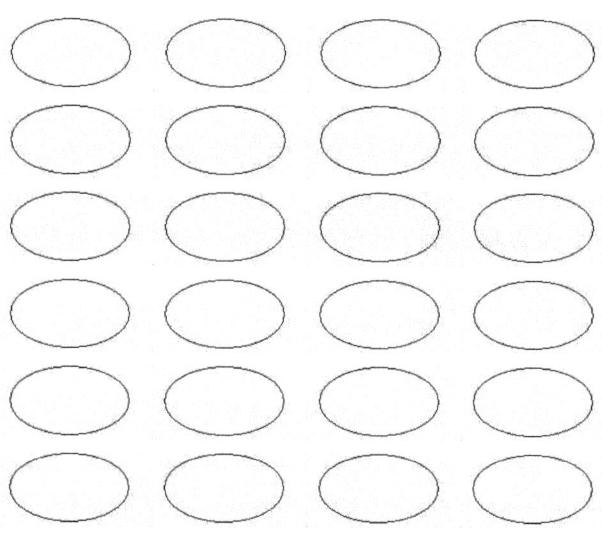

五、画影子

以下是 4 个常见的物体(正立方体、圆纸片、铅笔、圆锥体)。如果在夜晚用手拿着一个物体，使物体位于电灯的正下方，桌子的上方(如图。图中未画出拿物体的手)，则桌面上会有物体的影子。如果把物体任意转动，则物体影子的形状可能也会发生变化。请把每个物体在任意转动时可能出现的各种形状的影子画出来，画出影子的轮廓即可(手的影子不要考虑)。

1.正立方体　　　　2.圆纸片

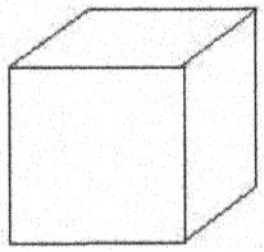

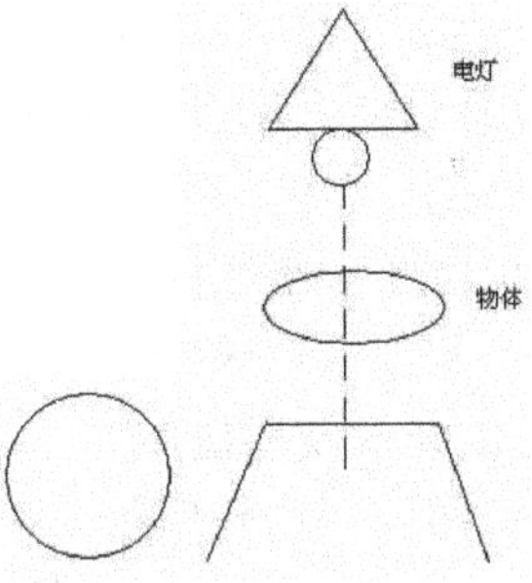

电灯

物体

3.铅笔　　　　4.圆锥体

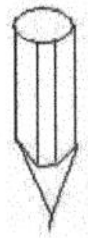

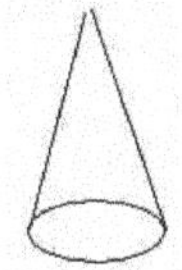

1. 正立方体的可能的影子形状：
2. 圆纸片可能的影子形状：
3. 铅笔可能的影子形状：
4. 圆锥体可能的影子形状：

Appendix III　The Questionnaire about Cognitive Ability

Name ________　Age ________　Sex ________　Level ________

Class ________

说明：感谢同学们参加这次问卷调查，对问卷中题目的回答不分对错，希望同学们根据自己的实际情况选择相应的选项。

1. 我知道语言中到处都存在隐喻。
   1）很符合　2）符合　3）一般　4）不符合　5）很不符合
2. 我知道英语文章中使用隐喻可以使语言表达更生动形象。
   1）很符合　2）符合　3）一般　4）不符合　5）很不符合

3. 英语课堂学习中我非常重视老师对隐喻的讲解。

    1) 很符合　2) 符合　3) 一般　4) 不符合　5) 很不符合

4. 在英语学习中遇到不懂的隐喻我会主动查字典以求其意。

    1) 很符合　2) 符合　3) 一般　4) 不符合　5) 很不符合

5. 在外教的课堂中,我感觉他们会经常使用隐喻。

    1) 很符合　2) 符合　3) 一般　4) 不符合　5) 很不符合

6. 我发觉中国英语老师讲课时也经常使用隐喻。

    1) 很符合　2) 符合　3) 一般　4) 不符合　5) 很不符合

7. 学习中我经常会比较英语和汉语隐喻的不同之处。

    1) 很符合　2) 符合　3) 一般　4) 不符合　5) 很不符合

8. 除了名词,我还会把其他词性也用作隐喻。

    1) 很符合　2) 符合　3) 一般　4) 不符合　5) 很不符合

9. 我知道隐喻也可以出现在句子层面上。

    1) 很符合　2) 符合　3) 一般　4) 不符合　5) 很不符合

10. 我现在很清楚,英语中有些隐喻概念和汉语不同。

    1) 很符合　2) 符合　3) 一般　4) 不符合　5) 很不符合

11. 我现在很清楚地知道,英语中有些隐喻语言表达式和汉语不同。

    1) 很符合　2) 符合　3) 一般　4) 不符合　5) 很不符合

12. 在使用隐喻时,我的大脑里会马上闪现对比对象的形象。

    1) 很符合　2) 符合　3) 一般　4) 不符合　5) 很不符合

13. 我会有意识地在写作、对话中运用课堂学习的隐喻。

    1) 很符合　2) 符合　3) 一般　4) 不符合　5) 很不符合

14. 英语写作中,只要能直接表达清楚思想,我尽量不去使用隐喻。

    1) 很符合　2) 符合　3) 一般　4) 不符合　5) 很不符合

15. 英语写作中需要隐喻表达时,我总是在大脑里搜寻学过的隐喻来表达。

    1) 很符合　2) 符合　3) 一般　4) 不符合　5) 很不符合

16. 英语写作时我会把相应的汉语隐喻翻译成英语。

    1) 很符合　2) 符合　3) 一般　4) 不符合　5) 很不符合

17. 我经常尝试着用新的隐喻来表达自己的思想。

    1) 很符合　2) 符合　3) 一般　4) 不符合　5) 很不符合

18. 在使用隐喻时，我清醒地意识到不同文化之间存在差异。
   1) 很符合　2) 符合　3) 一般　4) 不符合　5) 很不符合
19. 阅读过程中我对文章中出现的隐喻很敏感。
   1) 很符合　2) 符合　3) 一般　4) 不符合　5) 很不符合
20. 阅读过程中遇到隐喻难以理解时，我会按照相关词的字面意思去推断其意义。
   1) 很符合　2) 符合　3) 一般　4) 不符合　5) 很不符合
21. 阅读过程中，我会结合上下文来理解隐喻。
   1) 很符合　2) 符合　3) 一般　4) 不符合　5) 很不符合
22. 阅读过程中遇到隐喻时，如果在汉语中找不到相应的隐喻概念时，我觉得就很难理解。
   1) 很符合　2) 符合　3) 一般　4) 不符合　5) 很不符合
23. 阅读时，我会对文章中出现的隐喻使用的恰当性进行评判。
   1) 很符合　2) 符合　3) 一般　4) 不符合　5) 很不符合
24. 阅读前我会预期文章中将出现隐喻现象。
   1) 很符合　2) 符合　3) 一般　4) 不符合　5) 很不符合
25. 在理解隐喻时，我的大脑里会马上闪现对比对象的形象。
   1) 很符合　2) 符合　3) 一般　4) 不符合　5) 很不符合
26. 学习中我经常会比较英语和汉语隐喻的相同之处。
   1) 很符合　2) 符合　3) 一般　4) 不符合　5) 很不符合
27. 我意识到使用隐喻可以表达一些非隐喻语言无法表达的现象。
   1) 很符合　2) 符合　3) 一般　4) 不符合　5) 很不符合
28. 我感觉外教使用的隐喻比中国英语教师多。
   1) 很符合　2) 符合　3) 一般　4) 不符合　5) 很不符合
29. 我知道隐喻可以出现在语篇层面上。
   1) 很符合　2) 符合　3) 一般　4) 不符合　5) 很不符合
30. 和英语本族语用英语交流时，我经常和他们讨论隐喻问题。
   1) 很符合　2) 符合　3) 一般　4) 不符合　5) 很不符合

Appendix IV The Metaphor Comprehension Test

Name ________ Age ________ Sex ________ Level ________
Class ________

Directions: Dear students, we would like you to read the following sentences and explain the meaning of the sentences in your own words. You can write your answers in either English or Chinese.

1. As the war progressed, attitudes on both sides hardened.
2. I wish father weren't so negative; he pours cold water on all my ideas.
3. We got wind of his resignation a week before it was announced in the newspapers.
4. The police decided to play cat and mouse when he saw the woman steal the dress in the store.
5. I don't like being made a monkey in front of my friends; don't play your jokes on me again when we have guests.
6. For many years he was sitting on thorns, he had never qualified as a doctor, although he cured many of his patients.
7. He was absolutely right. Unfortunately, he was talking to a brick wall.
8. I figure there is a sword hanging over their head, and that is pressure.
9. The leader crushed the rebellion with an iron hand.
10. Hearing the news, he was like a cat on a hot tin roof.
11. Alison returned, looking sheepish.
12. When the boss isn't here, I feel like a million dollars.
13. If you resign from the party, you will only be driving a nail into your coffin.
14. Some members of the government flew a kite about wage

control on television.

15. Mary made a clean breast of the matter to her boss.
16. Tom got a bloody nose when he argued with his schoolmate.
17. He was a sour and cruel man.
18. They found it a sight for sore eyes.
19. Jane thought he was the most pig-headed man she had ever met.
20. Our life is controlled by faceless politicians.

Appendix V The Metaphor Production Test

Name ________ Age ________ Sex ________ Level ________
Class ________

Directions: Dear students, we would like you to write a composition on the topic "Love" with no less than 200 words. You are encouraged to use metaphors in composition. Thank you for your cooperation!

Bibliography

[1] Albert, A. & J. Kormos. Creativity and narrative task performance: an explanatory study[J]. Language Learning, 2004, 54(2), 277-310.

[2] Bailey, R. Conceptual metaphor, language, literature and pedagogy[J]. Journal of Language and Learning, 2003, 1/2, 59-72.

[3] Bennet, B. When is a "pretty kettle of fish" a "red herring"? [J]. Modern English Teachers, 1994, 3(2), 19-21.

[4] Bialystok, E. & M. Frohlich. Variables of classroom achievement in second language learning [J]. The Modern Language Journal, 1978, 62/7: 327-336.

[5] Blasko, D. On the tip of the iceberg: who understands what about metaphor? [J]. Journal of Pragmatics, 1999, 31: 1675-1683.

[6] Blasko, D. & D, Briihl. Reading and recall of metaphorical sentences: Effects of familiarity and context[J]. Metaphor and Symbol, 1997, 12 (4), 261-285.

[7] Block, D. Who framed SLA research? Problem framing and metaphoric accounts of the SLA research process. In Cameron, L & Graham Low (eds.). Researching and Applying Metaphor [M]. Shanghai: Shanghai Foreign Language Education Press, 2001.

[8] Boers, F. Enhancing metaphoric awareness in specialized reading[J]. English for Specific Purposes, 2000a, 19, 137-147.

[9] Boers, F. Metaphor awareness and vocabulary retention[J]. Applied Linguistics, 2000b, 21/4: 553-571.

[10] Boers, F. Applied linguistics perspectives on cross-cultural variation in conceptual metaphor[J]. Metaphor and Symbol, 2003, 18/4, 231-238.

[11] Bowdler, B. & D. Gentner. Metaphor comprehension from comparison to categorization[J]. Proceedings of the Twenty-first Annual Conference of the Cognitive Science Society, 1999, 90-95.

[12] Brisard, F., S. Frisson & D. Sandra. Processing unfamiliar metaphors in a self-paced reading task[J]. Metaphor and Symbol, 2001, 16(1 & 2), 87-108.

[13] Brown, A. Metacognitive development and reading. In R. J. Spiro, B. Bruce & W. F. Brewer (eds). Theoretical Issues in Reading Comprehension[M]. Hillsdale, N. J.: Erlbaum, 1980.

[14] Brown, A. Metacognition, executive control, self-regulation, and other more mysterious mechanisms. In F. Weinert & R. Kluwe (eds)[M]. Metacognition, Motivation, and Understanding. Hillsdale, NY: Lawrence Erlbaum Associates, 1987.

[15] Brumfit, C. & K. Johnson. The Communicative Approach to Language Teaching [M]. Shanghai: Shanghai Foreign Language Education Press, 2001.

[16] Buchwald, A. Don't say "let's get together" to a foreigner. In S. K. Cohen (ed.). Building Reading Fluency: Words in Focus[M]. Singapore: Thomas Learning, 2000.

[17] Bullock, A. & S. Trombley. The Norton Dictionary of Modern Thought[M]. New York London: W.W. Norton & Company, 1999.

[18] Caballero, R. Metaphor and genre: the presence and role of metaphor in the building review[J]. Applied Linguistics, 2003, 24/2: 145-167.

[19] Cameron, L. Identifying and describing metaphor in spoken discourse data. In Cameron, L & Graham Low (eds.).

Researching and Applying Metaphor [M]. Shanghai: Shanghai Foreign Language Education Press, 2001.

[20] Cameron, L & Graham Low. Survey article: metaphor, language, teaching[M]. Cambridge: Cambridge University Press, 1999.

[21] Cameron, L & Graham Low. Researching and Applying Metaphor [M]. Shanghai: Shanghai Foreign Language Education Press, 2001.

[22] Chamot, A. & M. O'Malley. The cognitive academic language learning approach: A model for linguistically diverse classrooms[J]. The Elementary School Journal, 1996, 96/3: 259-273.

[23] Chang Zongli. A case study of metaphor in literary readings [J]. Nottingham Linguistic Circular, 2002, 17: 75-88.

[24] Charteris-Black, J. Metaphor and vocabulary teaching in ESP economics[J]. English for Specific Purposes, 2000, 19: 149-165.

[25] Charteris-Black, J. Second language figurative proficiency: a comparative study of Malay and English [J]. Applied Linguistics, 2002, 23/1:104-133.

[26] Chomsky, N. Aspects of the Theory of Syntax[M]. Cambridge: MIT Press, 1965.

[27] Coates, J. Women, Men and Language[M]. London: Longman Group UK Limited, 1993.

[28] Collins, V. L *et al*. Metacognition and its relation to reading comprehension: a synthesis of the research[EB/OL].[2005-10-10].
http://idea. uoregon. edu./ncite/documents/techrep/tech23. helm.

[29] Cook, G. & B. Seidlhofer. Principles & Practice in Applied Linguistics [M]. Shanghai: Shanghai Foreign Language

Education Press, 2000.

[30] Cooper, T. Processing of idioms by L2 learners of English [J]. TESOL Quarterly, 1999, Vol. 33, No. 2, 233-261.

[31] Cortazzi, M & L, Jin. Bridges to learning: metaphors of teaching, learning and language. In Cameron, L & Graham Low (eds.). Researching and Applying Metaphor [M]. Shanghai: Shanghai Foreign Language Education Press, 2001.

[32] Croft, W. Typology and Universals[M]. Shanghai: Shanghai Foreign Language Education Press, 2000.

[33] Cumming, A. Writing expertise and second language proficiency [J]. Language Learning, 1989, 39, 81-141.

[34] Danesi, M. The role of metaphor in second language pedagogy [J]. Rassegna Italiana di Linguistica Applicata, 1986, 18 (3): 1-10.

[35] Danesi, M. Recent research on metaphor and the teaching of Italian[J]. Italica, 1997, 71/4.

[36] Deignan, A, D. Gabrys and A. Solska. Teaching English metaphors using cross-linguistic awareness-raising activities [J]. ELT Journal, 1997, 51/4. Oxford: Oxford University Press.

[37] Deignan, A.D. Metaphor[M]. Hongkong: The Commercial Press,2001.

[38] Dickinson, L. Autonomy and motivation: a literature review [J]. In Dickinson and Wenden (eds.). System: An International Journal of Educational Technology and Applied Linguistics: Special Issue on Learner Autonomy, 1995, Vol. 23, 165-174.

[39] Ellis, R. The Study of Second Language Acquisition[M]. Shanghai: Shanghai Foreign Language Education Press, 1994.

[40] Fain, M. A. Metaphors for learning: a cognitive exercise for students[J]. Research Strategies, 2001, 18: 39-48.

[41] Fainsilber, L. & A. Ortony. Metaphorical uses of language in the expression of emotions [J]. Metaphor and Symbolic Activity, 1987, 2(4): 239-250.

[42] Fine, H. J. & B. Lockwood. Figurative language production as a function of cognitive style[J]. Metaphor and Symbolic Activity, 1986, 1(2): 139-152.

[43] Fitzgerald, T. Metaphors of Identity[M]. New York: State University of New York Press, 1993.

[44] Flavell, J. Metacognitive aspects of problem solving. In L. B. Resnick (ed), The Nature of Intelligence[M]. Hillsdale, NJ: Erlbaum, 1976.

[45] Forrest-Pressley, D. & T. Waller. Cognition, Metacognition and Reading[M]. New York: Springger-Verlag New York Inc, 1984.

[46] Gagne, C. Metaphoric interpretations of comparison-based combinations [J]. Metaphor and Symbol, 2002, 17 (3): 161-178.

[47] Gibbs, R. The Poetics of Mind: Figurative Thought, Language, and Understanding[M]. Cambridge: Cambridge University Press, 1994.

[48] Gibbs, R. Process and products in making sense of tropes. In Ortony, A (ed.). Metaphor and Thought[M]. Cambridge: Cambridge University Press, 1998.

[49] Gibbs, R. Researching metaphor. In Cameron, L & Graham Low (eds.). Researching and Applying Metaphor [M]. Shanghai: Shanghai Foreign Language Education Press, 2001.

[50] Gibbs, R. & G. Steen. Metaphor in Cognitive Linguistics[M]. Amsterdam: John Benjamins Publishing Company, 1997.

[51] Giora, R. Understanding figurative and literal language: the graded salience hypothesis[J]. Cognitive Linguistics, 1997, 7: 183-206.

[52] Giora, R. On the priority of salient meanings: studies of literal and figurative language[J]. Journal of Pragmatics, 1999, 31: 919-929.

[53] Giora, R. Literal vs. figurative language: different or equal? [J]. Journal of Pragmatics, 2002, 34: 487-506.

[54] Glicksohn, J. S. Kraemer & O. Yisraeli. A note on metaphoric thinking and ideational fluency [J]. Metaphor and Symbolic Activity, 1993, 8(1): 67-70.

[55] Glucksberg, S. Metaphors in conversation: How are they understood? Why are they used? [J]. Metaphor and Symbolic Activity, 1989, 4(3): 125-143.

[56] Glucksberg, S. & B. Keysar. How metaphor works. In Ortony, A (ed.). Metaphor and Thought [M]. Cambridge: Cambridge University Press, 1998.

[57] Goatly, A. The Language of Metaphors [M]. London: Routledge Taylor & Francis Group, 1997.

[58] Golden, L & O. Hardison. Aristotle's Poetics: A Translation and Commentary for Students of Literature[M]. New York: Prentice-Hall, Inc. Englewood Cliffs, N. Y, 1989.

[59] Gough. One second of reading. In Kavanagh & Mattingly (eds.), Language By Ear and By Eye[M]. Cambridge, Mass: MIT Press, 1972.

[60] Gould, M. The Problem of Metaphor in Philosophy of Mind [M]. National Library of Canada, 2002.

[61] Graham, S. Effective Language Learning [M]. Clevedon, Multilingual Matters, 1997.

[62] Grant, L. & L. Bauer. Criteria for re-defining idioms: Are we barking up the wrong tree? [J]. Applied Linguistics,

2004, 25(1): 38-61.

[63] Grube, G. Aristotle on Poetry and Style[M]. New York: Liberal Arts Press, 1958.

[64] Guerrero, M. & O. Villamil. Exploring ESL teachers' roles through metaphor analysis[J]. TESOL Quarterly, 2000, 34/2: 341-351.

[65] Gyori, G. Semantic change and cognition [J]. Cognitive Linguistics, 2002, 13(2): 123-166.

[66] Hakuta, K. & R. Diaz. The relationship between degree of bilingualism and cognitive ability: a critical discussion and some new longitudinal data. Children's Language [M]. Hillsdale NJ: L. Erlbaum, 1985.

[67] Halliwell, S. The Poetics of Aristotle: Translation and Commentary[M]. The University of North Carolina Press, 1987.

[68] Hamilton, C. Review of metaphor in cognitive linguistics[J]. Cognitive Linguistics, 2004, 15-1.

[69] Harris, R & T. Taylor. Landmarks in Linguistic Thought: The Western Translation from Socrates to Saussure [M]. Routlege, London and New York, 1989.

[70] Holme, R. Metaphor, language, learning, and affect. Humanising Language Teaching, 2001, (6). http://www.hltmag.co.uk/nov01/mart2.htm.

[71] Holyoak, K & P. Thagard. The analogical mind[J]. American Psychologist, 52, 35-44, 1997.

[72] Hymes, D. On Communicative Competence[M]. Philadelphia: University of Pennsylvania Press, 1971.

[73] Irujo, S. Don't put your leg in your mouth: Transfer in the acquisition of idioms in a second language [J]. TESOL Quarterly, 1986, 20, 287-304.

[74] Jiang Nan. Form-meaning mapping in vocabulary acquisition in a second language [J]. Studies in Second Language

Acquisition, 2002, 24: 617-637.

[75] Jiang Nan. Semantic transfer and its implications for vocabulary teaching in a second language[J]. Modern Language Journal, 2004a, 88: 416-432.

[76] Jiang Yajun. Metaphors the English language lives by[J]. English Today, 2002, 71, 18, 3, 55-64.

[77] Johnson, A. Comprehension of metaphors and similes: a reaction time study[J]. Metaphor and Symbolic Activity, 1996, 11(2), 145-159.

[78] Johnson, J. The Body in the Mind: The Bodily Basis of Meaning, Imagination and Reason [M]. Chicago: The University of Chicago Press, 1981.

[79] Johnson, J. Developmental versus language-based factors in metaphor interpretation [J]. Journal of Educational Psychology, 1991, 83, 470-483.

[80] Johnson, J. Metaphor interpretations by second language learners: children and adults[J]. The Canadian Modern Language Review, 1996, 53, 1.

[81] Johnson, J & T. Rosano. Relation of cognitive style to metaphor interpretation and second language proficiency. Applied Linguistics, 1993, 14, 159-175.

[82] Kasper, L. Assessing the meta-cognitive growth of ESL student writers. TESL-EJ (EJ-09), 1997. http://www.kyoto-su.ac.jp/information/tesl-ej/Ej09

[83] Kecskes, I. On my mind: Thoughts about salience, context and figurative language from a second language perspective [J]. Second Language Research, 2006, 22, 2, 219-237.

[84] Kecskes, I. & I. Cuenca. Lexical choice as a reflection of conceptual fluency[J]. International Journal of Bilingualism, 2005, Vol. 9, 1, 49-67.

[85] Kennedy, G. Aristotle on Rhetoric: A Theory of Civic

Discourse[M]. Oxford: Oxford University Press, 1991.
[86] Kellerman, E. A Break with Tradition[M]. Plenary Presentation, Paris: EUROSLA, 1998.
[87] Kimmel, M. Metaphor variation in cultural context: Perspectives from anthropology [J]. European Journal of English Studies, 2004, 8,3: 275-294.
[88] Kintsch, W. & A. Bowles. Metaphor comprehension: What makes a metaphor difficult to understand? [J]. Metaphor and Symbol, 2004, (6).
[89] Kittay, E. Metaphor: Its Cognitive Force and Linguistic Structure[M]. Oxford: Clarendon Press, 1989.
[90] Kondaiah, K. Metaphorical systems and their implications to teaching English as a foreign language [J]. Asian EFL Journal, 2004, 6 (1).
[91] LaBerge & Samuels. Toward a theory of automatic information processing in reading[J]. Cognitive Psychology, 1974, 6, 293-323.
[92] Lakoff, G. & M. Johnson. Metaphors We Live By [M]. Chicago: The University of Chicago Press, 1980.
[93] Lakoff, G. The contemporary theory of metaphor. In Ortony (ed.) Metaphor and Thought[M]. Cambridge: Cambridge University Press, 1998.
[94] Lakoff, G. & M. Johnson. Philosophy in the Flesh: The Embodied Mind and Its Challenge to Western Thought[M]. New York: Basic Books, 1999.
[95] Langacker, R. Foundations of Cognitive Grammar: Theoretical Perspectives, Vol. 2 [M]. California: Stanford University Press, 1987.
[96] Lazar, G. Using figurative language to expand students' vocabulary[J]. ELT Journal, 1996, 50/1: 43-51.
[97] Lee, J. & D. Schallert. The relative contribution of L2

proficiency and L1 reading ability to L2 reading performance: a test of the threshold hypothesis in an EFL context[J]. TESOL Quarterly, 1997, 31, 713-736.

[98] Li Fuyin. The acquisition of metaphorical expressions, idioms, and proverbs by Chinese learners of English: a conceptual metaphor and image schema based approach[D]. Michigan: ProQuest Information and Learning Company, 2002.

[99] Lindstromberg, S. Vocabulary teaching in the light of an awareness of metaphor: a few ways of working[C]. IATEFL Conference Brighton, 1997.

[100] Li, Shuyun & Hugh Munby. Metacognitive strategies in second language academic reading: A qualitative investigation[J]. English for Specific Purposes, 1996, 50/3: 199-216.

[101] Littlemore, J. Metaphoric intelligence and foreign language learning[J]. Humanising Language Teaching, 2001a, 3: 1-8.

[102] Littlemore, J. Metaphor competence: A language learning strength of students with a holistic cognitive style[J]. TESOL Quarterly, 2001b, 353: 459-491.

[103] Littlemore, J. The use of metaphor in university lectures and the problems that it causes for overseas students[J]. Teaching in Higher Education, 2001c, 6(3), 333-349.

[104] Littlemore, J. The effect of cultural background on metaphor interpretation[J]. Metaphor and Symbol, 2003, 18(4), 273-288.

[105] Littlemore, J. & G. Low. Metaphoric competence, second language learning, and communicative ability[J]. Applied Linguistics, 2006, 27, 2, 268-294.

[106] Livinston, J. Metacognition: an overview[M/OL]. 1997. http://www.gse.buffalo.edu/fas/shuell.

[107] Lopez, B. The Use of Metaphors as Metacognitive Devices in SLA and Learner Autonomy [M]. University of Las Americas Puebla. Ex-Hacienda de Santa Catarina Martir, Cholula, 2001.

[108] Low, G. On teaching metaphor[J]. Applied Linguistics, 1988, 9/2: 125-147.

[109] Low, G. Validating metaphor research projects. In Cameron, L & Graham Low (eds.). Researching and Applying Metaphor [M]. Shanghai: Shanghai Foreign Language Education Press, 2001.

[110] MacLennan, C. Metaphors and prototypes in the learning and teaching of grammar and vocabulary[J]. International Review of Applied Linguistics, 1994, XXXII/1: 97-110.

[111] Mahon, J. Getting your sources right: What Aristotle didn't say. In Cameron, L & Graham Low. 2001. Researching and Applying Metaphor [M]. Shanghai: Shanghai Foreign Language Education Press, 2001.

[112] Martinez, F. Exploring figurative language proficiency in bilinguals: the metaphor interference effect [D]. Thesis submitted to the Office of Graduate Studies of Texas A&M University, 2003.

[113] Martinich, A. The Philosophy of Language[M]. Oxford: Oxford University Press, 1990.

[114] McCabe, A. Effect of different contexts on memory for metaphor[J]. Metaphor and Symbolic Activity, 1988, 3 (2), 105-132.

[115] McGlone, M. Conceptual metaphors and figurative language comprehension: food for thought? [J]. Journal of Memory and Language, 1996, 35, 544-565.

[116] Moser, K. Metaphor analysis in psychology—method, theory, and fields of application. Forum: Qualitative Social

Research, 1/2, 2000.

[117] Murphy, G. On Metaphoric representation[J]. Cognition, 1996, 60: 173-204.

[118] Nickerson, R. S. The Teaching of Thinking[M]. Hillsdale, NJ: Lawrence Erlbaum Associates, 1985.

[119] Ortony, A. Metaphor and Thought[M]. Cambridge: Cambridge University Press, 1998.

[120] Osherson, D. The study of cognition. In Gleitman, L. M, Liberman (ed.) [M]. An Invitation to Cognitive Science, Vol. 1: Language 2nd Edition[M]. Cambridge, Mass: The MIT Press, 2000.

[121] Otto, I. The relationship between individual differences in learner creativity and language learning success[J]. TESOL Quarterly, 1998, 32 (4), 763-773.

[122] Paivio, A. & M. Walsh. Psychological processes in metaphor comprehension and memory. In Ortony (ed.), Metaphor and Thought [M]. Cambridge: Cambridge University Press, 1998.

[123] Paul, L. Approaches to the teaching of idiomatic language. International Review of Applied Linguistics in Language Teaching, 1998, 36/1.

[124] Picken, J. Metaphor in narrative and the foreign language learner[R]. Nottingham Circular, 16, 2001.

[125] Ponterotto, D. Metaphors we can learn by: How insights from cognitive linguistic research can improve the teaching/learning of figurative language [R]. English Teaching Forum, 32/3, 1994.

[126] Popova, Y. "The fool sees with his nose": Metaphoric mappings in the sense of smell in Patrick Suskind's Perfume [J]. Language and Literature, 2003, 12(2): 139.

[127] Preston, D. Socio-linguistics and Second Language Acquisition

[M]. Cambridge, Mass: Basil Blackwell Inc, 1989.

[128] Rakova, M. The Extent of the Literal Metaphor, Polysemy and Theories of Concepts[M]. Beijing: Beijing University Press, 2003.

[129] Reyan, V. & B. Kiernan. Children's memory and metaphorical interpretation[J]. Metaphor and Symbol, 1995, 10 (4): 309-331.

[130] Reynolds, R. & A. Ortony. Some Issues in the measurement of children's comprehension of metaphorical language[J], Child Development, 1980, 51: 1110-1119.

[131] Richards, A. The Philosophy of Rhetoric [M]. Oxford: Oxford University Press, 1965.

[132] Robinson, P. Individual differences, cognitive abilities, aptitude complexes and learning conditions in second language acquisition[J]. Second Language Research, 2001, 17/4: 368-392.

[133] Rohrer, T. The cognitive science of metaphor from philosophy to neuropsychology. Metaphor and Neuropsychology [J/OL]. 1995. http:// D: metaphor % and %20 Neuropsychology.htm

[134] Roth, R. The Role of Transfer in the Comprehension of L2 Idioms: A comparison of Advanced and Intermediate Students [D], 1997.

[135] Sardinha, T. Metaphor in corpora: a corpus-driven analysis of applied linguistics[R]. Applied Linguistics Postgraduate Program. Catholic University of Sao Paulo, Brazil, 2002.

[136] Saygin, A. Processing figurative language in a multi-lingual task: translation, transfer and metaphor [R]. In Proceedings of Corpus-Based & Processing Approaches to Figurative Language Workshop, Corpus Linguistics. Lancaster University, 2001.

[137] Scaruffi, P. Thinking about thought[J/OL], 2006. http:// www. thymos. com/tat/ metaphor.html

[138] Searle, J. Metaphor, Meaning and Expression. Cambridge: Cambridge University Press, 1978.

[139] Searle, J. Metaphor. In Ortony (ed.), Metaphor and Thought [M]. Cambridge: Cambridge University Press, 1998.

[140] Semino, E, J., Heywood & M, Short. Methodological problems in the analysis of metaphors in a corpus of conversations about cancer [J]. Journal of Pragmatics, 2004, 36, 1271- 1294.

[141] Sjostrom, S. From vision to cognition: A study of metaphor and polysemy in Swedish. In Allwood, J. & P. Gardenfors (ed.), Cognitive Semantics: Meaning and Cognition [M]. John Benjamins Publishing Company, Amsterdam and Philodephia, 1998.

[142] Sperber & Wilson. Relevance: Communication and Cognition [M]. Shanghai: Shanghai Foreign Language Education Press, 2001.

[143] Steen, G. Understanding Metaphor in Literature: An Empirical Approach[M]. London: Longman, 1994.

[144] Steen, G. Metaphor and language and literature: a cognitive perspective[J]. Language and Literature, 2000, 9: 261-277.

[145] In Hamilton. Current Issues in Linguistic Theory[J]. Book Reviews Cognitive Linguistics, 2004, 15-1: 104-111.

[146] Stefanowisch, A. The function of metaphor: Developing a corpus-based perspective [J]. International Journal of Corpus Linguistics, 2005, 10 (2): 161-168.

[147] Stern, H. Fundamental Concepts of Language Teaching [M]. Shanghai: Shanghai Foreign Language Education Press, 1983.

[148] Sternberg, R. *et al*. Metaphor, induction, and social policy: the convergence of macroscopic and microscopic views. In

Ortony (ed.), Metaphor and Thought[M]. Cambridge: Cambridge University Press, 1998.

[149] Sticht, T. Educational uses of metaphor. In Ortony (ed.), Metaphor and Thought [M]. Cambridge: Cambridge University Press, 1998.

[150] Svorou, S. The Grammar of Space[M]. Amsterdam: John Benjamins, 1994.

[151] Sweetser, E. From Etymology to Pragmatics: Metaphorical and Cultural Aspects of Semantic Structure[M]. Beijing: Beijing University Press, 2003.

[152] Thornbury, S. Metaphors we work by: EFL and its metaphors [J]. ELT Journal, 1991, 45/3.

[153] Turner, M. Reading Minds: The Study of English in the Age of Cognitive Science[M]. Princeton, NJ: Princeton University Press, 1991.

[154] Ungerer, F. & H. Schmid. An Introduction to Cognitive Linguistics[M]. Beijing: Foreign Language Teaching and Research Press, 2001.

[155] Vann, R. & R. Abraham. Strategies of unsuccessful language learners[J]. TESOL Quarterly, 1990, Vol. 24, 177-198.

[156] Waggoner, J., D. Palermo & S. Kirsh. Bouncing bubbles can pop: contextual sensitivity in children's metaphor comprehension [J]. Metaphor and Symbol, 1997, 12 (4), 217-229.

[157] Wales, K. Metaphor identification [J]. Language and Literature, 2002, Vol. 11.

[158] Walsh, C. From "capping" to intercision: metaphors/metonymys of mind control in the young adult fiction of John Christopher and Philip Pullman [J]. Language and Literature, 2003, 12(3): 233-251.

[159] Wang, Wenyu & Wen, Qiufang. L1 use in the L2 composing process: an exploratory study of 16 Chinese EFL writers[J].

Journal of Second Language Writing, 2002, 11(2): 225-246.

[160] White, M. Metaphor and economics: the case of growth[J]. English for Specific Purposes, 2004, 22, 131-151.

[161] Wilkins, D. Linguistics and Language Teaching[M]. London: Edward Arnold, 1972.

[162] Willis, J & D. Willis. Challenge and Chance in Language Teaching [M]. Shanghai: Shanghai Foreign Language Education Press, 2002.

[163] Wu, Su Yueh. A preliminary examination of teachers college students' difficulty with English idioms through their translation[J]. Nanjing Normal Uriversity Journal, 2003, 37, 1-16.

[164] Yamashita, J. Mutual compensation between L1 reading ability and L2 proficiency in L2 reading comprehension[J]. Journal of Research in Reading, 2002, 25, 80-94.

[165] Yang Yonglin. A Socio-Cognitive Study of Chinese Students' Color Codability in English[M]. Beijing: Qinghua University Press, 2002a.

[166] Yu, Ning. The Contemporary Theory of Metaphor: A Perspective from Chinese [M]. Amsterdam/Philadephia: John Benjamins Publishing Company, 1998.

[167] Yu, Ning. Metaphor, body, and culture: the Chinese understanding of gallbladder and courage[J]. Metaphor and Symbol, 2003, 18 (1): 13-31.

[168] 蔡龙权.关于把隐喻性表达作为外语交际能力的思考[J].外语与外语教学,2005,6: 21-25.

[169] 陈嘉映.语言哲学[M].北京:北京大学出版社,2003.

[170] 戴炜栋等.简明英语语言学教程[M].上海:上海外语教育出版社,1998.

[171] 桂诗春.外语教学的认知基础[J].外语教学与研究,2005,4: 243-249.

[172] 胡壮麟.认知隐喻学[M].北京:北京大学出版社,2004.

[173] 蒋楠.外语概念的形成和外语思维[J].现代外语,2004,4:378-385.

[174] 姜亚军,张辉.国外隐喻与第二语言习得研究述评[J].外语研究,2003.

[175] 姜孟.英语专业学习者隐喻能力发展实证研究[J].国外外语教学,2006,4:27-34.

[176] 蓝纯.从认知角度看汉语和英语的空间隐喻[M].北京:外语教学与研究出版社,2003.

[177] 马广惠.影响二语写作的语言因素研究[M].南京:河海大学出版社,2004.

[178] 庞继贤,丁展平.隐喻的应用语言学研究[J].外语与外语教学,2002,6:9-12.

[179] 皮亚杰,王宪钿译.发生认识论原理[M].北京:商务印书馆,1997.

[180] 束定芳.隐喻学研究[M].上海:上海外语教育出版社,2003.

[181] 束定芳.语言的认知研究:认知语言学论文精选[M].上海:上海外语教育出版社,2004.

[182] 王寅,李弘.体验哲学和认知语言学对词汇和词发法成因的解释[J].外语学刊,2004,2:1-6.

[183] 吴红云,刘润清.二语写作元认知理论构成因子分析[J].外语教学与研究,2004,3:187-195.

[184] 杨小虎,张文鹏.元认知与中国大学生英语阅读理解相关研究[J].外语教学与研究,2002,3:213-218.

[185] 杨永林.是范式的交替,还是方法的变换?— 外语学科中范式理论应该缓行[J].现代外语,1999,4:420-427.

[186] 杨永林.社会语言学研究:功能,称谓,性别篇[M].上海:上海外语教育出版社,2004.

[187] 张厚粲.瑞文标准推理测验在我国的修订[J].心理学报,1989,21/3.

[188] 赵艳芳.认知语言学概论[M].上海:上海外语教育出版

社,2002.

Acknowledgements

As I looked back at the process of writing this dissertation, I came to realize that there are many people that I want to thank. However, due to space limitation, I can only single out a few. First of all, I want to express my gratitude to my dissertation advisor, Professor Wang Tongshun, for his meticulous critiquing of my ideas and my analysis of the data, which resulted in significant improvement in the quality of this dissertation. Being one of his many students in its real sense has provided with me a precious opportunity to be exposed to his unforgettable tutelage of various kinds, academic and non-academic.

My special thanks should go to Professor Yang Huizhong, Professor Wang Dechun, Professor Zheng Shutang, Professor Pan Wenguo, Professor Wei Naixing, Professor Yu Liming, Professor Chen Yongjie, Professor Wang Zhenhua, Professor Jin Yan, Professor Tian Yan, Professor He Xiaofen, for their academic and professional guidance.

I am also most grateful to Professor Yang Yonglin, my MA advisor, Dr. Zhou Aibao, Dr. Wu Shiyu for their sensible and constructive suggestions for the experimental design and statistics of the present research.

I would also like to express my sincere thanks to Mr. Michael Barron, Mr. Peter Marlarky, Ms. Emily Myers, Ms. Zhoulin for their careful and meticulous work into evaluating the subjects' protocols.

I am greatly indebted to my students who volunteered to be the subjects in my experiment for their collaborative work.

My colleagues at Shanghai Institute of Technology shared my teaching load while I was on leave for this dissertation. I want to thank them all for being a great supportive team. I have a few friends who have stood by me through thick and thin. To Professor Gao Xiang, Dr. Wang Guoyong, Dr. Mu Congjun, Dr. Zhang Daqiu, I want to express my profound gratitude for their moral support over the years

I have been blessed by the enduring love of my parents, my sister and my brothers.